101 Things I Learned in Culinary School

101 Things I Learned® in Culinary School

Second Edition

Louis Eguaras with Matthew Frederick

CROWN
NEW YORK

CROWN and the Crown colophon are registered trademarks of Penguin Random House LLC.

101 Things I Learned is a registered trademark of Matthew Frederick.

Originally published in the United States in slightly different form by Grand Central Publishing,
a division of Hachette Book Group, New York, in 2010.

Library of Congress Cataloging-in-Publication Data

Names: Eguaras, Louis, author. | Frederick, Matthew, author.
Title: 101 things I learned in culinary school / Louis Eguaras, Matthew
Frederick.
Other titles: One hundred and one things I learned in culinary school
Description: Second edition. | New York: Crown, 2020. | Series:
101 thingsI learned | Includes bibliographical references and index.
Identifiers: LCCN 2019037360 (print) | LCCN 2019037361 (ebook) | ISBN
9781524761943 (hardcover) | ISBN 9781524761950 (ebook)
Subjects: LCSH: Cooking—Study and teaching. | Cooks—Training of.
Classification: LCC TX661 .E58 2020 (print) | LCC TX661 (ebook) | DDC
641.5071—dc23
LC record available at https://lccn.loc.gov/2019037360
LC ebook record available at https://lccn.loc.gov/2019037361

ISBN 978-1-5247-6194-3

Ebook ISBN 978-1-5247-6195-0

Printed in China

randomhousebooks.com

9 8 7 6 5 4 3 2 1

First Crown Edition

Illustrations by Matthew Frederick

Cover illustration by Matthew Frederick

From Louis
To Agnes, for believing in me, for everything.

Authors' Note

Since the first edition of this book was published, the culinary world has evolved at a remarkable pace, thanks largely to the growth of food-related websites, television programs, recipe generators, cooking apps, prepared meal delivery systems, and—we like to think—books like this one.

A field that has always demanded the mastery of so much information and so many skills has gotten even more complicated. When there is so much to learn, where does one begin?

Right here. We have packed this new edition with useful advice, hard-earned wisdom, and informational frameworks to get you started in the kitchen—or maybe more accurately, to prepare you to start. Whether you are buying pots, selecting potatoes, or grilling a porterhouse, this book will help you figure out what is most important to know, and will help organize your learnings.

If you are an experienced cook, you will find within many reminders and insights that will keep you grounded in best practices. And if you are pursuing a career in the field, you will learn about critical aspects of the culinary profession— how chefs think and conduct themselves, how a professional kitchen works, and the terminology and procedures that keep a restaurant running smoothly.

Like the first edition, this is not a recipe book. While it will teach you a bit about how to cook, more than anything we want it to help you get *ready* to cook. So keep this small volume in the kitchen for reference. Or put it on your coffee table, in your toolbox, or in your jacket pocket to peruse in your free moments. It can be read randomly, so dip in anywhere at any time—between classes, on the bus, or while waiting for water to boil. Use it as a friendly reminder and refresher. And now that you have this second edition in hand, feel free to use the first edition as a coaster.

Louis Eguaras and Matthew Frederick

Acknowledgments

From Louis
Thanks to my mother, Maridel Gonzalez-Beckman; my stepfather, Kent M. Beckman; Steve Brown; Stephen Chavez; Jeffrey Coker; Mark Diamond; Ronald Ford; Monica Garcia-Castillo; Peter George; Martin Gilligan; Herve Guillard; Simon Harrison; Keith Luce; Mike Malloy; Jayson McCarter; Roland Mesnier; John Moeller; Glenn Ochi; Patrice Olivon; Mike Pergl; Mauro Daniel Rossi; Lachlan Sands; Walter Scheib; Mike Shane; Paul Sherman; Trinidad Silva; Richard Simpson; Rick Smilow; Robert Soriano; Bruce Whitmore; Matthew Zboray; my chef instructor colleagues, who appreciate the simple explanation of culinary techniques and terminology; my students for being a resource of what to present in this book; the United States Navy; and, most importantly, my beautiful wife and best friend, Agnes Castillo Jose-Eguaras.

From Matt
Thanks to Ty Baughman, Sorche Fairbank, Matt Inman, and Josephine Proul.

101 Things I Learned in Culinary School

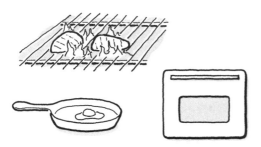

Dry cooking
direct heat or oil

Moist cooking
water-based

There are only two ways to cook.

Dry cooking directly exposes food to heat, using radiation, convection, or oil. Methods include sautéing, pan-frying, deep-frying, grilling, broiling, roasting, and baking. It produces browning or searing of the food's surface.

Moist cooking transfers heat to food via immersion in water or a water-based liquid, such as milk, wine, or vegetable stock. Methods include boiling, simmering, poaching, and steaming. Foods are not browned and are usually tender when done.

In *sous vide* (soo veed, French for "under vacuum"), a food is sealed in plastic or glass and heated for a long time in hot water. This makes it an "in-between" method in which the water does not contact the food despite being the heating medium. In braising and stewing, dry and moist cooking are typically combined by first searing meat with dry heat, then simmering it at length in liquid.

Cookware
measured across the top

Bakeware
measured across the bottom

Don't buy a matched set of pots.

Cast iron: Very heavy, which allows it to heat evenly and maintain very high temperatures, making it ideal for browning/searing. Durable, but reactive to acids, thus requiring frequent seasoning (a protective layer of fat and carbon) to prevent rust. Enameled cast iron does not have to be seasoned, but it can chip and discolor.

Stainless steel: Lightweight, nonreactive to acids, and not a good heat conductor. Make sure a layer of aluminum or other highly conductive material is included in the pot base to promote heat transfer.

Aluminum: Lightweight, inexpensive, and a good heat conductor, but reactive to acids and easily dented. Anodized aluminum is less reactive and more durable.

Carbon steel: Durable, heats quickly, requires regular seasoning. Good for woks, paella pans, and crêpe pans.

Copper: Best conductivity and most even heating; responsive to temperature changes. Expensive, reactive to acids, tarnishes quickly. Popular for making sauces and sautéing.

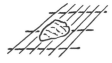

Grill
directly exposes
food to fire

Sauciér
sauces, custards, risotto,
creamy foods; whisking

Sauté pan
braising, pan-frying

Griddle
a continuous flat
heating surface

Skillet
browning, caramelizing;
reducing sauces

Saucepan
basic heating and
boiling

A griddle is not a grill.

Griddle: a heavy piece of cooking equipment with a continuous flat heating surface. Often used for pancakes, eggs, omelets, cheesesteaks, and other diner-type foods.

Grill: an open web that allows food to be directly exposed to fire. Most useful in cooking meats and some fish and vegetables.

Saucepan: has a squared cross section, used for basic heating and boiling.

Saucér: has a tapered cross section and rounded bottom, suiting it to preparing sauces, custards, risotto, and other creamy foods, as there are no corners in which food can hide and burn. Additionally, its shape accommodates whisking.

Skillet: has low, flared sides that help dissipate moisture. It is useful for pan-frying, browning/caramelizing, and reducing sauces. The sloped sides make it easy to flip food and slide it out when done.

Sauté pan: useful for pan-frying but has straight, high sides and a lid to reduce splatters and keep in heat and moisture. Especially useful in combination cooking, for example when pan-browning a food before transitioning to moist cooking.

A restaurant kitchen is a military operation.

A restaurant kitchen is not a professional version of a home kitchen. It is a highly ordered production system in which all activities are interrelated. Every food item and scrap has a plan. Every dish is prepared with a specific outcome in mind, to match the vision of the head chef. Success requires strict adherence to the chain of command established by the kitchen brigade system.

Executive chef: In charge of every aspect of the kitchen, including menu, recipes, supplies, equipment, vendors, and staffing. Often acts as expeditor.

Expeditor: Performs the final check on plates to verify that each matches the standards and vision of the executive chef. Wipes smudges, adds garnishes, coordinates with servers.

Sous chef: Second in charge; typically an executive chef in training. Hires and schedules personnel, may act as expeditor.

Station chefs/line cooks: Directly prepare food upon order by guests. Typically work at one kitchen station, e.g., sauces, grill, sauté, fish, fry, roast, vegetables, or *garde manger* (preparer of cold foods); may fill in at other stations. Report to sous chef.

Prep cooks: Perform advance preparation for line cooks, such as measuring ingredients; cutting meats, seafood, vegetables, and fruits; monitoring soups and sauces.

Kitchen lingo

All day: total number of items to be prepared, e.g., 2 burgers rare + 1 burger medium = "3 burgers all day."

Check the score: Tell me the number of tickets that need to be prepared.

Down the Hudson: into the garbage disposal

Dragging: not ready with the rest of the order, e.g., "The fries are dragging."

Drop: Start cooking, e.g., "Drop the fries."

Family meal: a meal prepared for kitchen staff to eat, prior to or after a shift

Fire: Start cooking, but with more urgency, e.g., "Fire the burgers."

Get me a runner: Find someone to take this food to a table now.

In the weeds: running behind

Make it cry: Add onions.

The Man: the health inspector (whether male or female)

On a rail or on the fly: with extreme urgency, e.g., "Get me two soups on the fly."

Mise en place is a practice *and* a philosophy.

Before beginning direct preparation of a dish or starting a work shift, determine everything you will need. Gather recipes, ingredients, utensils, pots, pans, stocks, sauces, oils, serviceware, and anything else. Perform all advance preparation and arrange everything in the order in which you will use them when cooking begins.

Effective *mise en place* (meez ahn plahs, French for "putting in place") permits the most efficient use of a cook's space and time. It allows one to work in a state of constant readiness without stopping to search for or assemble essential items. But more than a mode of preparation, *mise en place* is a philosophy that informs the disposition and posture of the chef; how and where food, pots, and utensils are stored; the movement of foods from arrival through storage, preparation, plating, and table delivery; and even cleanup and waste. *Mise en place* should infuse the entire kitchen environment and the mindsets of those within it.

"The universe is in order when your station is set up the way you like it: you know where to find everything with your eyes closed, everything you need during the course of the shift is at the ready at arm's reach, your defenses are deployed."

—ANTHONY BOURDAIN (1956–2018),
Kitchen Confidential

Call it out!

"Knife!" "Behind you!" "Hot pan!" "Open oven!" "Corner!" Communications must be called out clearly and promptly in a busy kitchen; a polite "excuse me" isn't enough. A failure to communicate effectively can result in someone being burned, cut, or tripped, or dropping what they are carrying.

Paring knife: 2" to 4" blade, used to cut fruits and vegetables.

Boning knife: 5" to 7" firm blade, used to remove meat from a carcass.

Fillet knife: 5" to 8" pliable blade, straight or curved, used for filleting fish.

French (chef's) knife: 8" to 14" blade; versatile knife used for chopping, slicing, dicing, and mincing.

Serrated slicer: 12" to 14" jagged, toothed blade, typically used to cut bread but also tomatoes and pineapples.

Five knives will do 95% of the work.

Cooks often must buy their own knives to take with them from job to job. It's better to buy fewer, higher-quality knives than more, inexpensive ones, as they require less effort to use and are less likely to slip and break.

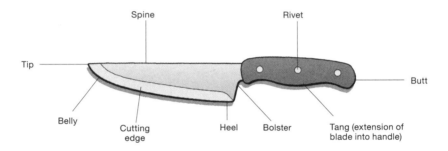

Spine

Rivet

Tip

Butt

Belly

Cutting
edge

Heel

Bolster

Tang (extension of
blade into handle)

Anatomy of a knife

Knife blades are most often made of stamped or forged metal. Stamped blades are made by using a template to cut a flat piece of metal. Forged knives are crafted with extreme heat to temper the steel. Stamped knives are lighter and less expensive, but lack the quality and balance of forged knives and don't maintain sharpness as well.

Carbon steel blade: a mixture of carbon and iron. Often used for chef's knives because it is easy to sharpen, although it is readily discolored by acidic foods.

Stainless steel blade: the most common material in kitchens. It does not corrode or discolor and can last longer than carbon steel, but does not hold as sharp an edge.

High-carbon stainless steel blade: Preferred by many chefs because it does not corrode or discolor, and is easy to sharpen.

Ceramic blade: Molded and fired from powdered zirconium oxide, a material second in hardness only to diamonds. Extremely sharp, rustproof, easy to maintain and clean, and nonreactive to acids, but easier than the others to chip.

Yes

No

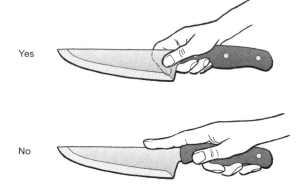

Shake hands with a knife.

To hold a chef's knife properly, rest your thumb on one side at the juncture of the blade and handle, and let your middle, ring, and pinkie fingers grip the handle naturally on the other side. The index finger rests on the side of the blade, near the handle. "Choking up" in this way will give you maximum control and minimize strain on the wrist—a critical consideration when working all day in the kitchen.

Never rest your index finger atop the blade, pointing down its length. While this might seem to lend stability, it will actually increase wobbling and rob your strokes of power and accuracy.

Rectangular

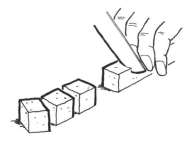

Dice

Cut fork foods 2½" or smaller.

The **basic cuts** a cook must master are as follows.

Dice cuts: suitable for vegetables such as carrots, celery, onions, root vegetables, and potatoes, for use in soups, stews, stocks, and sides.

> **Brunoise** (broo-NWAZ) / small dice: $1/8$" x $1/8$" x $1/8$"
>
> **Macédoine** (mah-se-DWAN) / medium dice: $1/4$" x $1/4$" x $1/4$"
>
> **Parmentier** (par-men-ti-AY) / large dice: $1/2$" x $1/2$" x $1/2$"

Rectangular cuts: thin, matchstick-like strips roughly square in cross section, often used for vegetables, meats, and fish for sautéing and stir-frying.

> **Fine julienne** (joo-lee-ENN): $1/16$" x $1/16$" x $2^1/2$" long
>
> **Julienne:** $1/8$" x $1/8$" x $2^1/2$" long
>
> **Batonnet:** (bah-toh-NAY): $1/4$" x $1/4$" x $2^1/2$" long

Cuts longer than $2^1/2$" are usually avoided because they are difficult to fit into the mouth.

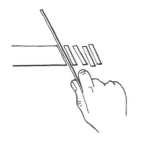

Bias or Asian

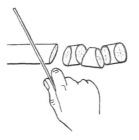

Oblique or Roll

Chiffonade

Paysanne

Rondelle

Tourné

Specialty cuts

Bias or **Asian:** a diagonal cut, often used for elongating slices of slender vegetables; more surface area enables faster cooking.

Oblique (oh-BLEEK) or **Roll:** made in the manner of a bias cut, but the food is rolled a partial turn between each cut, producing an irregular "V" shape. Good for vegetables in stocks and roasting, as it maximizes surface area.

Chiffonade (shif-uh-NAHD): a thin, shred-like cut used for leafy herbs and greens. The leaves are stacked, rolled into a cylinder, and thinly sliced.

Paysanne (pie-ZAHN): a flat, square cut, about $\frac{1}{2}$" x $\frac{1}{2}$" x $\frac{1}{8}$" thick. Used most often as a garnish.

Rondelle (ron-DELL): flat, round slices cut from vegetables or fruits, primarily used in soups, salads, and side components.

Tourné (tor-NAY): a football- or barrel-shaped cut for potatoes, carrots, and other root vegetables, $1\frac{1}{2}$" long x $\frac{1}{2}$" inch wide, with 7 facets around and blunt ends.

E. coli

The temperature spectrum

°F	°C	
0	−18	freezer
40	4	refrigerator
41–135	5–57	food danger zone; bacteria can double in 20 minutes
90	32	most fats begin to melt
110	43	tolerable maximum for hands in water for a short time
120	49	standard setting for residential hot water heater
140–165	60–74	general minimum safe-to-eat range for meats
145–170	63–77	slow cooker "warm" setting
160–180	71–82	water temperature for poaching
165	74	safe internal temperature for stuffing, casseroles, leftovers
171	77	minimum water temperature for sanitizing
180	82	water temperature for commercial dishwasher rinse cycle
185–205	85–96	water temperature for simmering
212	100	water boils at sea level and becomes steam
240	116	kills most microbial cells in dormant state
250–350	121–177	food surface temperature for browning most foods
350–375	177–191	oil temperature for deep-frying
350–520	177–271	smoke point range for most cooking oils
357	181	food surface temperature at which most foods begin to burn
625–800	329–427	commercial pizza oven

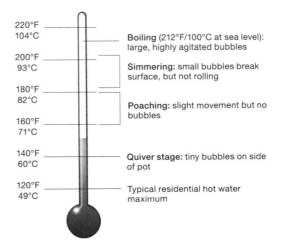

220°F
104°C

Boiling (212°F/100°C at sea level): large, highly agitated bubbles

200°F
93°C

Simmering: small bubbles break surface, but not rolling

180°F
82°C

Poaching: slight movement but no bubbles

160°F
71°C

140°F
60°C

Quiver stage: tiny bubbles on side of pot

120°F
49°C

Typical residential hot water maximum

How to boil water

1   Fill a comfortably sized pot with a generous amount of water; too much is better than too little. Cold water is preferred to help foods added prior to boiling, such as rice, eggs, and root vegetables, cook more evenly.

2   Place the pot on the stove and cover with a lid. Don't use a burner or flame larger than the pot, to avoid wasting energy.

3   Add salt *after* boiling begins to prevent pitting of aluminum and cast iron pots, but well before adding food to help it dissolve and penetrate the food. Water for pasta, potatoes, and vegetables should be very salty (about a teaspoon per quart of water), as only some will be absorbed into the food and most will be poured off. But be much more conservative in salting water for rice, beans, and grains, as most or all will be absorbed by the food.

1

2

How to calibrate a mechanical thermometer

Electronic thermometers are preferred for many uses, but traditional thermometers are still valued in the kitchen. They should be calibrated at least once a week and whenever dropped. To calibrate:

1   Fill a glass with crushed ice. Add cold water and stir thoroughly. Insert the thermometer so it does not touch the side or bottom of the glass.

2   When the dial stops moving (usually about 30 seconds), turn the calibration nut under the head so the pointer points precisely to 32°F/0°C.

3   Leave the thermometer untouched in the ice water for another 30 seconds. Verify that it is still pointing to 32°F/0°C, and adjust if required.

Alternatively, you can use boiling water and adjust the thermometer reading to match the boiling point at your altitude.

Random hypothesis: the most universal texture preference is a crisp outside and tender inside.

In our primitive state, we were hunters and gatherers, acting on a natural impulse to seek, engage, conquer, and enjoy. Nature provided many of the foods we crave with barriers against our urges: the shell of a nut, the skin of a fruit, the hide of an animal. These barriers increase our struggle but ultimately enhance our enjoyment.

Our civilized engagement with food re-creates our natural state through a cultivated process of denial and reward. Whether we are baking bread, searing vegetables, browning a steak, or caramelizing the surface of crème brûlée, we are reliving and elevating our primitive culinary desires.

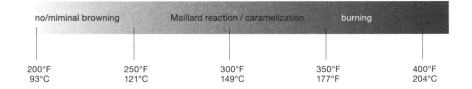

no/miminal browning   Maillard reaction / caramelization   burning

| 200°F | 250°F | 300°F | 350°F | 400°F |
| 93°C | 121°C | 149°C | 177°F | 204°C |

Approximate food surface temperatures

Brown it.

Two different, but related, browning reactions occur when a food is heated to a surface temperature between about 250 and 350°F (121–177°C). In foods with naturally occurring sugars and certain amino acids, such as meat or bread, it is the **Maillard reaction**. In fruits and vegetables, which have natural sugars but not the critical amino acids, it's **caramelization**.

Considerable fuss is often made over this distinction, but in practice there is little reason to be concerned with which is occurring. They're *both* browning. Whether searing, sautéing, frying, roasting, grilling, broiling, griddling, or toasting, and whether the food is a starch, protein, or green vegetable, browning will tend to maximize flavor, provide a crisp outside, and preserve a tender inside.

Blister/char, sear,
stir-fry, sauté

Pan-fry

Deep-fry

Oil levels

Deep-fry at 350 to 375°F (177 to 191°C).

Blister/char/sear: uses a minimal amount of oil and very high heat (425°F/218°C and up) for 1 to 2 minutes per side to brown the surface of a food without moving it. This may be done as either an introductory process before transitioning the food to a simmer or braise, or a finishing process after the main cooking has been completed.

Stir-fry: Cook small meats and vegetables by keeping them moving quickly with high heat (400–425°F/204–218°C) and a little bit of oil.

Sauté: Brown a food in a medium-hot (275–350°F/135–177°C), lightly oiled pan. Food may then be simmered in the same pan by adding moisture, covering, and reducing heat.

Pan-fry: Use $1/8$" to $1/2$" of oil, so food is submerged no more than halfway, and a medium-high to high temperature (350–400°F/177–204°C).

Deep-fry: Fully immerse food in oil at 350–375°F/177–191°C. A higher temperature risks burning the food; lower won't achieve a crisp, light exterior. Cook in small batches to maintain oil temperature. Remove food debris to avoid lowering the smoke point.

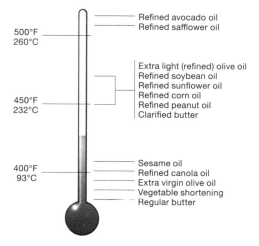

Refined avocado oil
Refined safflower oil

500°F
260°C

Extra light (refined) olive oil
Refined soybean oil
Refined sunflower oil
Refined corn oil
Refined peanut oil
Clarified butter

450°F
232°C

Sesame oil
Refined canola oil
Extra virgin olive oil
Vegetable shortening
Regular butter

400°F
93°C

Approximate smoke points

Pan rules

1 Heat the pan before adding oil when blistering/charring, searing, stir-frying, or sautéing. If you put oil in too early, the chemical bonds in the oil will break down too soon and it will lose its lubricating properties. Pan-frying and deep-frying are exceptions because of the greater volume of oil.

2 Add oil only when the pan is hot. Use an oil with a smoke point at least 25°F/14°C higher than the anticipated pan temperature. The smoke point is when an oil begins to break down and burn. Be especially attentive to the flame if using butter or extra virgin olive oil, which have fairly low smoke points.

3 If the oil smokes or changes color before you add food, it's too hot. Throw away the oil, clean the pan, and start over. Otherwise the oil will release carcinogens and may reach the flash point, when it combusts.

4 Use dry, room-temperature food.

5 Never crowd the pan.

6 To minimize sticking of proteins (meat, eggs, fish), don't flip prematurely. A protein that is satisfactorily seared will tend to naturally release from the pan.

Stir-fry is a form of sautéing that uses a wok.

Make a sauté jump.

In French, *sauté* literally means "jump": the pan must be hot enough to cause food placed in it to jump or pop. For a successful sauté:

- Use thorough *mise en place*, as timing is critical.
- Make sure all foods are dry.
- Use a large, lightly oiled pan. Crowding will minimize contact of food with the heat source and cause undesirable moisture to build up, preventing browning.
- Heat the pan without oil, until a few drops of water tossed on it sizzle.
- Place a small amount of oil in the pan and continue heating. You can tell the pan is hot enough by tossing a small piece of onion into it. If it jumps, it's ready.
- Add food and keep it moving fast. Root vegetables such as carrots take the longest. Put mushrooms, shrimp, and scallops in later to prevent them from getting rubbery.
- Learn to do a pan flip, which turns more food than a spatula, promoting more even cooking.

1

2

3

4

How to do a pan flip

22

1   "Shimmy" the pan or nudge the food with a wooden spoon to make sure it isn't sticking.

2   Lift the pan and tilt the far edge aggressively downward so the food slides away from you.

3   Just before the food slides out, quickly lift the far edge to direct the food upward and slightly back toward you. The food will become airborne.

4   Move the pan slightly away from you to catch the food in the center. Work on timing, so the completion of this step loads into the initial movement of another flip. But be careful not to remove the pan from the heat source for too long.

Novices should practice with a cold pan and a slice of toasted bread before risking injury or wasted food with a hot pan.

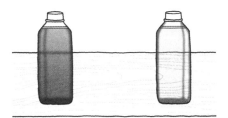

Unrefined oils	**Refined oils**
created by directly pressing a food (e.g., olive, peanut, walnut)	extracted at high temperatures, often with the use of chemicals
may be cloudy or have sediment	pure-looking product; clear and light
maintain presence of source; strong flavor, color, aroma	processing makes them less flavorful and nutritious
more suited to low-temperature cooking	higher smoke point than unrefined counterpart
best used where their flavor is valued, e.g., salad dressings, sauces	best used in dishes in which oil is not needed for flavor, e.g., baking
include cold pressed, expeller pressed, and expeller cold pressed	long shelf life, but added deodorizers may mask rancidity

Three oils will handle almost everything.

For general cooking, choose an oil that is nonallergenic and has an adequate smoke point.

23

Canola oil has a smoke point of 400°F/204°C, which suits it to most high-heat cooking. It is inexpensive, and its neutral flavor makes it good for baking.

Olive oil is healthful and has a great, nuanced flavor. Extra virgin olive oil has a fairly low smoke point of 320 to 390°F/160 to 199°C, making it risky for some cooking uses. Refined olive oil has less flavor but a smoke point as high as 485°F/252°C.

A finishing or table oil is needed to accompany cold foods, such as salads and bread. Extra virgin olive oil and walnut oil are popular choices. Many other oils are available, and may complement specific dishes, but are unlikely to be as versatile. Infused oils have had a flavor added, such as garlic, basil, or chili.

Whichever oils you choose, make sure they suit the character of the menu and the individual dishes on it. Butter, lard, oils, and other fats will lend markedly different characters to food.

"This beautiful, approachable book not only teaches you how to cook, but captures how it should *feel* to cook: full of exploration, spontaneity and joy. Samin is one of the great teachers I know." —Alice Waters

SALT FAT ACID HEAT

MASTERING THE ELEMENTS OF GOOD COOKING

by SAMIN NOSRAT

and art by WENDY MacNAUGHTON

with a foreword by MICHAEL POLLAN

"When we think of France, we think of butter. When we think of Italy or Spain, we think of olive oil. When we think of India, we think of ghee. If I was trying to make something that tasted Japanese at home, I wouldn't use olive oil because . . . it will never taste properly Japanese. So to make the thing taste of the place, start with the fat of the place."

—SAMIN NOSRAT

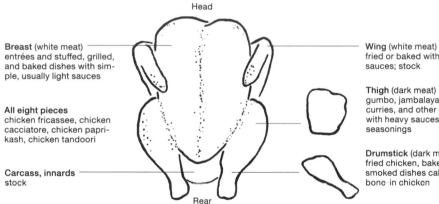

24

Head

Breast (white meat) entrées and stuffed, grilled, and baked dishes with simple, usually light sauces

All eight pieces chicken fricassee, chicken cacciatore, chicken paprikash, chicken tandoori

Carcass, innards stock

Rear

Wing (white meat) fried or baked with sauces; stock

Thigh (dark meat) gumbo, jambalaya, fajitas, curries, and other dishes with heavy sauces or seasonings

Drumstick (dark meat) fried chicken, baked and smoked dishes calling for bone-in chicken

Leg

What to do with a whole chicken

Buying a whole bird opens up culinary potential and saves money. To fabricate a bird, follow its natural structure to locate the bones and joints.

Wing: Point the rear of the bird toward you. For most uses, remove the wing at the joint closest to the body. If preparing airline-style breasts, leave the first wing bone attached to the breast, and sever the wing at the middle joint. You can leave the meat on the wing or push it toward the breast.

Leg: Pull away from the bird and begin cutting where the leg meets the breast. Continue downward toward the thigh joint. Bend the leg toward you and twist until the thighbone pops out of the joint. Cut the meat below and around the leg, following the rib cage and backbone. Trim carefully around the oyster meat, located next to the backbone, so it stays attached to the thigh.

Separating drumstick and thigh: Place the whole leg skin-side down. Wiggle the leg parts and feel where they meet at the joint. Cut straight through at the joint.

Breast: Following the line of the breastbone, carve out the breast meat on each side, cutting close to the rib cage.

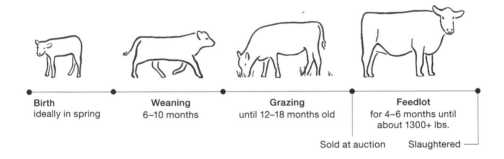

Birth
ideally in spring

Weaning
6–10 months

Grazing
until 12–18 months old

Feedlot
for 4–6 months until
about 1300+ lbs.

Sold at auction   Slaughtered

Common timeline for commercial beef

Good beef is a month old.

Meat from animals such as lambs, pigs, and poultry is aged after slaughter for a very short time and often not at all. But cattle, being larger and older, must be aged to allow the animal's natural enzymes to break down its tougher tissues.

In **dry aging,** beef is hung and exposed in refrigerated air for anywhere from about two weeks to a few months. The meat loses 15 to 30% of its weight, mostly due to water evaporation, and develops more intense flavor. Dry-aged beef is considered a premium product and is rarely found in supermarkets.

In **wet aging,** beef is vacuum packed in plastic in its own juices for 5 to 7 days. The final product is more mildly flavored and less expensive than dry-aged beef. If the method is not labeled on a package of beef, it was almost certainly wet-aged.

	Lowest quality ⟵ ⟶ Highest quality			
Grade:	Standard, Commercial, Utility, Cutter, Canner	**USDA Select**	**USDA Choice**	USDA PRIME
Marbling:	n.a.	3 to 4%	4 to 7%	8 to 11%
Comments:	Suitable for ground beef, meat pies, meat sticks, potted meats	About ⅓ of graded beef. Popular at retail, but usually the lowest grade in restaurants	More than half of all graded beef	Awarded to 2% of graded beef. Rare in supermarkets, sold mostly to restaurants

USDA quality grades

Prime doesn't necessarily mean "best."

27

A cut of beef might be described as "prime," but only a label of "USDA Prime" indicates that it meets the highest industry standard. The USDA inspects separately for **wholesomeness** and **quality**. Wholesomeness inspection is mandatory and is publicly funded. Quality inspection is performed upon the request of, and is funded by, cattle producers and meat packers. Quality grades are based on marbling (greater distribution of flecks and streaks of fat = more tender, juicy, and flavorful), color, and age (cattle 18 to 24 months old are considered best).

Higher-quality meats tend to be more suited to dry cooking, lesser cuts to moist cooking.

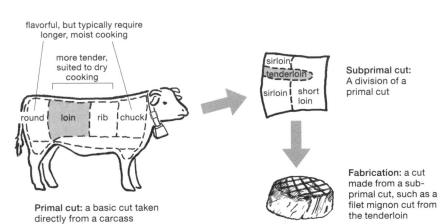

flavorful, but typically require longer, moist cooking

more tender, suited to dry cooking

round   loin   rib   chuck

sirloin
tenderloin
sirloin   short loin

Subprimal cut: A division of a primal cut

Fabrication: a cut made from a sub-primal cut, such as a filet mignon cut from the tenderloin

Primal cut: a basic cut taken directly from a carcass

The tender parts are in the middle.

A simple mnemonic device makes it easy to remember which meat cuts come from which parts of an animal: Round is from the rump, and chuck is from the shoulder. Between them are the loin and rib.

Chuck: about 28% of carcass weight. Flavorful, but with many connective tissues calling for moist or combination cooking. Not used in food service as much as other primal cuts. In veal and lamb, it is called shoulder; in pork, shoulder or butt.

Rib: about 10% of carcass weight. Heavily marbled and very tender. Suited to dry or combination cooking. In veal, lamb, and pork, it is called the rack.

Loin: short loin and sirloin together make up 15% of the carcass. Very tender; most of the popular and expensive cuts come from the loin. Excellent for dry cooking.

Round: 24% of carcass weight. Very flavorful, moderate connective tissues, best roasted/braised. In veal, lamb, and pork, it is called the leg.

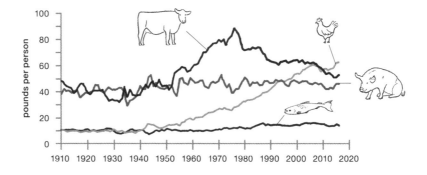

28

U.S. per capita availability of meat and fish, 1910–2016
Source: USDA

Four ways to tenderize

Mechanical: Pound with a mallet before cooking.

Marinade: Use an acidic bath (buttermilk, lemon or lime juice, tomato juice, vinegar, or yogurt) for 30 minutes to 2 hours. Or marinate in a puree of kiwi, papaya, pineapple, or Asian pear, which contain tenderizing enzymes. To avoid mushiness, halt if the meat edges start to look gray or cooked. Avoid room-temperature marinating, and never use a marinade after cooking.

29

Salting/brining: Thoroughly coat a dry piece of meat with coarse salt and refrigerate it for 1 to 4 hours. The salt initially extracts moisture; then the protein fibers take back the salty juices for a more tender, flavorful product. Before cooking, rinse off the salt and pat the meat thoroughly dry. Brining works similarly; use $1/2$ cup salt per gallon of water.

Slow cooking: Cook a tough cut, such as brisket, chuck, or shoulder, at a low temperature for a long time in liquid in a slow cooker, stovetop pot, or oven.

If a cooked piece of meat remains tough, score or slice it across the grain before serving. For the diner, the meat will break apart more easily along its natural fiber lines.

1 Touch the tip of varying numbers of fingers to the thumb on the same hand.

To approximate:

Rare: Use a relaxed hand (don't touch fingers to thumb)

Medium rare: Touch index finger to thumb

Medium: Touch first 2 fingers to thumb

Medium well: Touch 3 fingers to thumb

Well done: Touch all 4 fingers to thumb

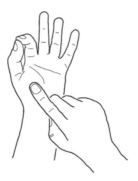

2 Feel the fleshy area at the base of the thumb with the index finger of your other hand. The area's firmness will approximate that of beef from rare to well done.

The hand comparison test for beef doneness

Recognizing beef doneness

30

A good cook can visually and intuitively recognize meat doneness, an important skill when taste-testing or cutting into a food is prohibited. Developing this skill takes much trial and error. In beef steaks, interior doneness is as follows:

Rare: very red and cool to slightly warm

Medium rare: red and warm

Medium: pink and fully warm

Medium well: grayish-brown with a hint of pink, and hot

Well done: grayish-brown and fully hot

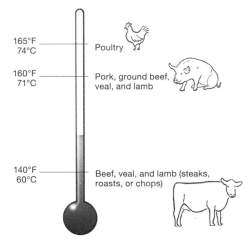

165°F
74°C — Poultry

160°F
71°C — Pork, ground beef,
veal, and lamb

140°F
60°C — Beef, veal, and lamb (steaks,
roasts, or chops)

Minimum safe-to-eat internal temperatures for meats

Food keeps cooking after you stop cooking.

31

After a food is removed from a heat source, its outer portions radiate heat into the air of the kitchen. Meanwhile, some of the food's heat conducts more deeply into its interior. Consequently, a food's internal temperature—particularly in thick meats—may rise for several minutes. During this period, the meat continues to cook.

Allow for **carryover cooking** in meats by removing them from the heat source when the internal temperature is about 5°F/3°C below the safe-to-eat temperature. Monitor the internal temperature as small and medium cuts sit for 5 to 10 minutes, large cuts for as long as 20 minutes.

Par-cook
with salt by boiling or steaming; stop before fully done, when color turns vivid.

Shock
the food in an ice water bath to quickly arrest cooking.

Drain
and store for later use, or serve cold/at room temperature.

Flash reheat
before serving by boiling, broiling, sautéing, or grilling.

Blanching

Finish cooking

Start cooking before you start cooking.

At dinner hour a kitchen may have only 15 minutes to prepare an appetizer or entrée—an impossibly narrow window for most foods. Par-cooking allows a food to be mostly cooked well in advance of order, quickly cooled to arrest cooking, and stored. Finish cooking is done upon order. This not only improves timing, but yields many other benefits:

32

Finish cooking can be flexible. A large quantity of a food, such as chicken breasts, may be baked or steamed at the beginning of the day, and later grilled, broiled, or sautéed for different dishes.

Cooking methods can be combined for best outcomes. French fries, for example, may be par-boiled for fluffiness and later deep-fried for a crispy exterior.

Overcooking of leftovers is eliminated, because one is not reheating a fully cooked food.

Catering burdens are eased when cooking facilities in remote venues are limited.

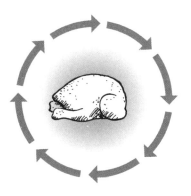

Why convection ovens are faster

33

When a cool food is placed in an oven, it absorbs heat and the oven air around it cools. In a conventional oven, this air is replaced only gradually by warmer air.

A convection oven works by rapidly moving air, thereby continually replacing the cooled air next to the food with air at the ideal temperature. The result is faster, more even cooking at 25 to 50°F/14 to 28°C below the temperature called for in a conventional oven.

All ovens tend to have a lower temperature near the door. This differential is also reduced in a convection oven because of continual air replacement.

Very low-fat fish	Low-fat fish	Medium-fat fish	High-fat fish
< 2g	2–5g	5–10g	≥ 10g

usually lighter, flakier, milder   usually darker, firmer, more flavorful

clams, cod, crab, **haddock,** lobster, mahi-mahi, scallops, shrimp, sole, tuna	**halibut,** mussels, ocean perch, oysters, tilapia, pink salmon	bluefish, catfish, **rainbow trout,** swordfish	herring, mackerel, **sardines;** Atlantic, Coho, sockeye, and Chinook salmon

Fat per 3 oz. in selected fish
(farm-raised counterparts may have more fat)

Fresh fish smells like the water it came from. Old fish smells like fish.

34

Fresh fish looks and smells clean and has a sweet, water-like scent. It should have no slime, cuts, or bruises, and the fins should be pliable. When selecting fish:

- Run your fingers across the scales. If they separate easily, it is not fresh.
- There should be some tightness or resistance when you press gently on the fish.
- The eyes should be clear, shiny, and clean, and not sunken below the head.
- The gills should be bright pink or bright red, not dark red or gray.
- Check for "belly burn," a dark reddish, bloodlike stain on the skin, which indicates that the viscera were left in the fish too long, resulting in bacteria growth.

Crustaceans

semi-transparent exoskeleton

two-part body—cephalothorax and abdomen

segmented (jointed) appendages

include barnacles, crab, crayfish, lobster, shrimp/prawn

Mollusks

usually hinged, calcareous shell

generally undifferentiated body

muscular foot or tentacles for movement

include clam, cockle, cuttlefish, loco, mussel, octopus and squid (no shell), oyster, periwinkle, scallop, snails

Shellfish

Frozen shrimp are the freshest shrimp.

35

When shrimp are offered for sale as "fresh," they almost certainly were flash-frozen at sea and later thawed. However, blind tests show that most consumers prefer frozen seafood over fresh. In an extensive study funded by the National Fish and Wildlife Foundation, identical meals were prepared from fresh and frozen fish, and consumer preferences were evaluated through blind tests. Consumers rated the frozen fish equal or superior to fresh fish in all categories. Scientific examination found that the cell structure in the fish that had been frozen was much healthier.

5 to 6 qts. cold water
unsalted

5 lbs. bones
roasted (for brown
stock) or unroasted
(for white stock)

1 lb. vegetables
$\frac{1}{2}$ onions, $\frac{1}{4}$ celery, and $\frac{1}{4}$
carrots (brown stock) or $\frac{1}{4}$
leeks or parsnips (white stock)

Seasoning
bay leaf, peppercorns,
garlic, and parsley

Stock ingredients

Don't boil or salt stock.

Every time you carve a carcass, have a plan in place to maximize its potential. The most readily available opportunity is stock, which may be used as the basis for many sauces, soups, stews, gravies, and glacés. **White stock** is made from unroasted bones and vegetables. **Brown stock** is derived from bones and vegetables that were roasted in the oven to enhance their flavor.

Cook vegetable and fish stocks 45 minutes to 1 hour, poultry stock 4 to 8 hours, and veal stock 8 to 48 hours. Don't use any salt, as subsequent reduction may make the stock too salty. Instead, add salt when preparing the final product from the stock. Also, avoid boiling, as this may break down the ingredients too much and make the stock cloudy. Maintain a gentle simmer, and regularly skim any impurities that rise to the top.

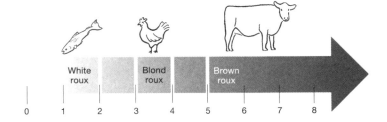

36

White roux

Blond roux

Brown roux

0 1 2 3 4 5 6 7 8

Cooking time for roux, in minutes

How to thicken a stock, soup, or sauce

Reduction: Remove the pan lid and simmer until desired thickness is achieved. A preferred method for many cooks, as it intensifies the native flavor of a dish.

Roux: Heat butter or other fat in a saucepan. Slowly add an equal weight of flour, stirring constantly to produce a paste. The longer the roux is heated, the darker and more flavorful it will be, although the less thickening power it will have.

37

Slurry: Mix a powdered product with cold water or stock until smooth, and slowly add to the sauce. Corn or potato starch is good for dairy-based, but not acidic (e.g., tomato) sauces; is gluten-free; and yields a mostly clear product. Kudzu and arrowroot powders freeze well and are good for acidic sauces. Wheat flour is fairly versatile, but will make a clear broth or sauce opaque.

Egg yolk: Suits dessert sauces and cream-based savory sauces. Requires tempering (slowly adding hot or warm sauce to the egg) so the egg doesn't scramble.

Gelatin: Good for both sweet and savory; entirely flavorless and crystal clear. Thickens more as it cools. May unfavorably alter texture in some instances.

Marie-Antoine Carême (1784–1833)

The five mother sauces

Marie-Antoine Carême, the founder of classical French cuisine, identified four "mother sauces" to be made in large quantities. Auguste Escoffier later adapted this list to create the five mother sauces used in kitchens today. From them, daughter sauces are created through additions such as spices, herbs, or wine.

38

Béchamel (cream) sauce: base of milk and white roux. Suited to pasta, fish, and chicken. Daughter sauces include Mornay, Nantua, Soubise, and Mustard.

Velouté (white) sauce: white stock/blond roux base, for fish and chicken entrées. Daughter sauces include Poulette, Aurora, Curry, Mushroom, and Albufera.

Espagnole (brown) sauce: brown stock/brown roux base, suitable for poultry and meat. Daughter sauces include Bordelaise, Robert, Chasseur, and Madeira.

Tomato sauce: tomato base, for pasta, poultry, and meat. May be flavored by rib bones and meats. Daughters include Bolognese, Creole, and Portuguese.

Hollandaise (butter) sauce: base of clarified butter, egg yolk, and lemon juice. Suits eggs and vegetables. Daughters include Maltaise, Mousseline, Noisette, and Girondine.

Butterhead
tender, sweet leaves; expensive; appealing in salads, sandwiches, lettuce wraps, and as bedding

Kale
healthful but tough; use very small pieces if serving raw

Arugula
long lasting; pungent, works with strong accompaniments such as tangy dressings and blue cheese

Spinach
dark leaves are good for counterpointing lighter greens, or use in spinach salad

Romaine or Cos
long lasting; popular in Caesar salad; most likely to have *E.coli*

Iceberg or Crisphead
inexpensive, crisp, clean tasting, shreds well; may need company of other greens for visual appeal

Leaf
red and green varieties; attractive ruffled edges; good "go-to" for salads and sandwiches

Popular salad greens

Rip, don't cut, salad greens.

Most greens fare better when ripped than when cut. Tearing encourages greens to break along natural fault lines. Cutting damages cells, producing bruising and browning.

Failproof balsamic vinaigrette
1 part vinegar
3 to 4 parts oil
$\frac{1}{4}$ part emulsifier

Emulsifiers

Emulsification is the combining of two immiscible (unmixable) liquids using rapid agitation to create a new liquid, such as a salad dressing of oil and vinegar. But left alone for just a few minutes, the mixture will separate. This problem can be solved by adding an emulsifier, such as egg yolk, mayonnaise, yogurt, ground nuts, mustard, or fruit puree, whose molecules are friendly to both water and fat.

Table
- highly refined
- additives may lend metallic taste
- fine granules promote consistent
  measurement, helpful in baking

Kosher
- not kosher per se, but
  used in koshering meats
- no additives
- granules vary in size
- coarse; easy to pinch
  and sprinkle

Sea
- evaporated from sea water
- strongest flavor
- expensive
- coarse or fine grains
- gray, pink, brown, black available

Rock
- large, unrefined crystals
- grayish hue
- not for eating, but often used in
  presenting shellfish

Common kitchen salts

Salt: when and when not to add

When tenderizing meat with salt, be sure to begin 1 to 4 hours before cooking.

When blanching, salt the water while par-cooking instead of waiting until flash reheating.

Add salt early in the cooking process. Salt heightens and blends other flavors. Adding it early gives you the best opportunity to evaluate and adjust.

When boiling water in an aluminum or cast iron pot, add salt after boiling begins but before adding food to prevent pitting of the pot material.

Don't salt immediately before deep-frying, as the salt will not adhere to the food and will be lost in the fryer.

Don't salt stock while making it, as subsequent reduction may make it too salty. Be similarly cautious in salting a sauce that will be reduced before plating.

Don't skimp on salt when following baking recipes. In baking, salt is specified not only for taste; it activates rising.

41

1 Melt butter in a heavy saucepan over medium heat. Water in the butter will evaporate and milk solids will settle to the bottom.

2 Strain the clarified portion into another container and discard the milk solids. One pound of regular butter produces about 12 liquid oz. of clarified butter.

Clarified butter

Unsalted butter in the kitchen, salted butter in the dining room.

Use unsalted butter in cooking and baking. The $1/3\pm$ teaspoon of salt and additional water in a stick of salted butter can alter recipe balance. Salted butter lasts longer, however, about 12 weeks versus 8 for unsalted.

Clarify butter to make it more buttery. Butter is about 80% fat. Removing the water and milk solids from unsalted butter results in a product that is 100% butterfat, which has more flavor, longer life, and a 100°F/56°C higher smoke point than regular butter. In Middle Eastern and Indian cooking, the clarified butter—called *sman* and *ghee,* respectively—is slightly browned, yielding a dark, nutty taste.

Mount the sauce with butter. Use the technique of *monter au beurre* (mon-tay o BURR, French for "mount with butter") by gently stirring a "knuckle" of cold, unsalted butter into a sauce just before serving. As it melts, the fat droplets will emulsify with the liquid in the sauce, giving it a velvety texture and rich sheen.

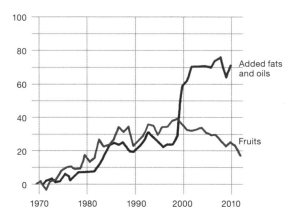

42

Percent change in average daily calories, U.S. adults
Source: USDA

Fat and cholesterol aren't the enemy.

The increases in obesity, type 2 diabetes, and other diet-related health problems in recent decades have often been blamed on fat and cholesterol in foods such as red meat, eggs, and butter. But studies indicate that naturally high-fat foods don't necessarily make people fatter; in fact, people on high-fat diets tend to eat fewer calories overall than their counterparts on low-fat diets. The more significant weight-loss variable appears to be protein: eating more of it leads naturally to reduced overall calorie consumption.

Nor is cholesterol in food necessarily harmful. The cholesterol in eggs, for example, does not raise blood cholesterol in otherwise healthy individuals.

Diet-related health epidemics are now thought by researchers to be primarily due to consumption of packaged foods, which are usually loaded with preservatives, artificial flavorings, trans fat, sugar, and corn syrup. Foods advertised as "low-fat" often have even more such additives to compensate for their lesser inherent flavor.

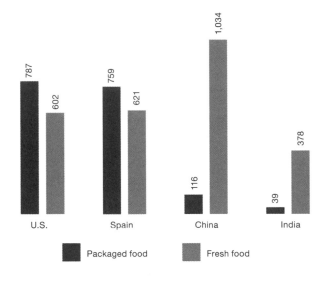

43

Per capita annual consumption of fresh and packaged food, in pounds
Sources: Euromonitor International and USDA Economic Research Service

"Every time you eat or drink you are either feeding the disease or fighting it."

—HEATHER MORGAN, NUTRITIONIST

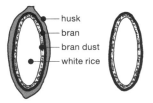

Paddy rice (unprocessed)	Brown rice (husk removed)	White rice (bran removed)	Enriched white rice

	Percent of available nutrients	Approximate nutrients available compared to brown rice	
Thiamin (B1)	100%	13%	106%
Magnesium	100%	22%	22%
Niacin (B3)	100%	25%	65%
Vitamin B6	100%	34%	34%
Folate	100%	35%	1,683%
Fiber	100%	36%	36%
Potassium	100%	46%	46%
Riboflavin (B2)	100%	52%	52%
Iron	100%	62%	334%
Protein	100%	95%	95%

husk — bran — bran dust — white rice

Rice: shorter = stickier

Rice is the seed of a type of grass. All rice begins as **brown rice,** the whole grain of rice from which only the husk has been removed. It has a nutty, hearty taste. **White rice** types include:

Long-grain (Indica) rice: firm and fluffy. It separates after cooking, suiting it to rice pilaf, fried rice, and steamed rice, but not risotto. Varieties include:
- **Basmati:** extremely aromatic. Grown in the Himalayan foothills, popular in Indian and Middle Eastern cuisines.
- **Carolina or Southern:** not aromatic. The most common rice in the United States.
- **Jasmine:** aromatic. Used in pilafs and Asian-style fried rice.

Short- and medium-grain (Japonica) rice: starchy, tender, and sticky. Good for risotto, sushi, and paella. Varieties include:
- **Arborio:** a round, medium grain with a mild flavor. Used primarily for risotto.
- **Calrose:** short and fat, commonly used in sushi in the United States.

Wild rice is not technically a member of the rice family, but like other rice is the seed of a type of grass. It is dark brown or black and has an earthy aroma and flavor. It takes three times longer to cook than most white rices.

45

High starch
low moisture/fluffy

Russet
Idaho
Goldrush
California Long White

Best for baking, roasting, mashing, frying, soup thickening

Yukon Gold
Yellow Finn
Peruvian Blue
Superior
Kennebec

OK for most uses

New
Red Bliss
Round White
Yellow

Best for potato salads, soups, casseroles

Low starch
high moisture/waxy

Potatoes: more starch = fluffier; less starch = better shape

If you're making a stew, potato salad, or potatoes au gratin, you want shape retention. Choose a **low-starch potato,** as its naturally high moisture content keeps it from absorbing too much water during moist cooking, allowing it to hold its shape. Low-starch potatoes are often small and round with a thin, waxy skin.

46

If you're baking, mashing, or deep-frying, you want fluffiness. Use **high-starch potatoes.** They aren't good for moist cooking because they absorb a lot of water, which can cause them to lose their shape. However, this makes them a good soup thickener.

All-purpose potatoes have medium starch. They are good for everything, although not exceptional for anything. **New potatoes** are any type of early or freshly harvested potatoes, whose sugars have not fully converted to starch. They perform in general like waxy potatoes.

		Cow	Goat	Sheep	Water buffalo
Softer	Cottage	P	-	-	-
↑	Ricotta	P	P	P	P
	Brie	P	-	-	-
	Camembert	P	-	-	-
	Fontina	P	-	-	-
	Mozzarella	s	s	s	P
	Port-Salut	P	-	-	-
	Cheddar	P	-	-	-
↓	Swiss	P	-	-	-
	Parmesan	P	-	-	-
Harder	Pecorino Romano	-	-	P	-

P = primary source   s = secondary source

Cheese: the younger, the softer; the softer, the meltier.

Cheese is made by adding acid or rennet (an enzyme from the stomach of some mammals) to milk, causing it to coagulate or curdle. Most cheeses are aged (ripened) from a few weeks to a year, while fresh or unripened cheeses, such as cream and cottage cheese, are not aged. The longer a cheese ages, the harder, drier, and more flavorful it tends to become, and the less it tends to melt. The hardest cheeses, such as Romano and Parmesan, melt only in small shavings. Cheese character is also affected by milk source:

Cow: Highest volume producer. Large fat globules are difficult for some to digest.

Goat: Small volume producer. Strongest flavor, more acidic and tart than cow. Molecular structure is close to human milk, making it easy to digest.

Sheep: Nearly twice the protein of cow and goat. High fat content makes it an excellent cheese source. More neutral tasting than goat.

Water buffalo: Production similar to goat; sweet flavor.

47

More elastic
(better for bread)

Protein content	Flour type
12–16%	**Bread and high-gluten flour:** from hard wheat. For bread, pizza dough, bagels, other chewy products. Browns well in the oven.
10–12%	**Whole wheat flour:** uses every part of the wheat kernel; richest in fiber and nutrients. Absorbs/needs more liquid. Highly perishable.
9–12%	**White/all-purpose (AP) flour:** blend of hard and soft wheat. Doesn't contain the bran and germ.
8–11%	**Self-rising flour:** AP flour to which salt and baking powder have been added. Not for yeast breads.
8–10%	**Pastry flour:** finely milled from soft wheat; flaky and tender product is perfect for pie crusts. DIY: use $1/3$ AP flour, $2/3$ cake flour.
5–8%	**Cake flour:** extra finely milled soft flour that yields a fine crumb. Also good for biscuits, muffins, scones.

Less elastic
(better for cake)

Bread needs chewy flour; cake needs crumby flour.

Protein content in wheat flour determines the amount of gluten and resulting elasticity. Hard red wheat produces flour high in protein and gluten, while soft red wheat yields lower gluten flours. Bread and pizza doughs need lots of elastic gluten strands to trap yeast gases, giving them their desired chewiness and air pockets. In cakes, a lower-gluten flour produces a finer, lighter crumb and minimal chewiness.

Semolina flour, from durum wheat, is an exception to the gluten/protein rule, as it is high in protein but not very elastic. It is ideal for pasta and couscous.

48

1 cup
AP flour

4.87 oz.±
138 g ±

1 cup
AP flour,
sifted

4.87 oz.±
138 g ±

1 cup
sifted
AP flour

4.48 oz.±
127 g ±

Sifted flour ≠ flour sifted

Weighing provides the most accurate measure.

In baking, slight deviations can cause dramatic failure. Flour types can vary in weight by as much as 1 ounce per cup. The wrong flour or too much of the right flour can produce a tough, dry product, while too little may cause a collapse.

When measuring flour, don't plunge a measuring cup directly into the flour sack, as this will compact it and you may end up with 20% more than intended. It's better to use a small scoop and gently spill several scoopfuls into a measuring cup that is exactly 1 cup to the brim. When it reaches overflowing, level it off with a knifo. However, even this method can produce widely varying results. The most dependable method is weighing.

49

Egg measurement can also be challenging. USDA egg sizing is based on the weight of a dozen, not the weight or size of each egg. A dozen large eggs (the size presumed by most recipes) must weigh 24 ounces. But individual eggs within it can vary significantly. Before cracking them, verify their weight against the 2-ounce average.

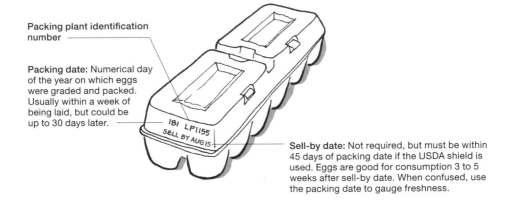

Packing plant identification number

Packing date: Numerical day of the year on which eggs were graded and packed. Usually within a week of being laid, but could be up to 30 days later.

181 LP1155
SELL BY AUG 15

Sell-by date: Not required, but must be within 45 days of packing date if the USDA shield is used. Eggs are good for consumption 3 to 5 weeks after sell-by date. When confused, use the packing date to gauge freshness.

Egg dating

The fresher the egg, the more flavorful and colorful its yolk and the better its white will hold its shape.

In savory cooking, the texture and flavor of eggs are often most important, while in baking their natural adhesive properties help bind other ingredients. Freshness also promotes volume, and helps guard against potentially harmful bacteria, especially in desserts in which eggs might not be adequately heated, such as crème anglaise, buttercreams, and mousses

Animal diet also affects flavor and quality. Free-range chicken eggs are more vibrant and flavorful than eggs from chickens fed a generic cornmeal diet.

50

Sweet   Sour   Salty   Bitter

Oohmommy

Tasteful definitions

Aroma: one's personal experience of a food as transferred from sense receptors in the nose to the brain. Common descriptors include grassy/green (green pepper); fruity (banana, apple); buttery (cheese); and woody/smoky (cinnamon, bacon).

Flavor: an inherent characteristic of a food, experienced through a combination of the senses of taste, touch, and smell.

Flavor profile: the qualities and combinations of flavors experienced when tasting a food, such as intensity, character, complexity, contrast, seasoning, the order in which flavor layers are noticed, aftertaste, and overall impression.

51

Mouthfeel: the physical sensation of a food in the mouth, exclusive of taste, although influenced by and influential on it. May include texture, chewiness, feel (e.g., light, velvety), density, grain, moistness, mouthcoating, and uniformity.

Palate: one's ability and sophistication in recognizing, distinguishing, and appreciating subtle variations in flavor, aroma, and texture.

Taste: one's personal experience of flavor; a sensation transferred to the brain from sense receptors (taste buds) on the tongue.

Taste categories: sweet, sour, salty, bitter, and umami. *Umami* is Japanese for, roughly, "meaty" or "savory."

1 Add a little stock, water, or wine to a pan containing "fond" (bits of caramelized food) left over from cooking.

2 Gently dislodge the fond with a wooden spoon.

3 Heat until the liquid reduces to the desired thickness. Serve as a flavorful sauce.

Deglazing

Focus the flavor.

Counterpoint: Use sweet, cool, or creamy foods to counterpoint spicy foods, such as mango salsa with spicy jerk chicken, or cool sour cream with 5-alarm chili. Try counterpointing crunchy with creamy, tart with smoky, and acidic with fatty.

Deepen: Reduce (boil down/evaporate) a sauce or deglaze a pan after sautéing to bring deeper flavor to a dish.

Intensify: Foods such as sesame seeds and pine nuts can be pan toasted to intensify their flavor before adding them to a main dish. Toast whole, fresh spices such as cumin before you grind them.

52

De-sour: If a dish is too sour, adding salt may "distract" the tongue and send it in search of sweeter notes.

Moderate: To keep a very strong-flavored food, such as seafood in a risotto, from dominating other flavors in the same dish, par-cook it separately and add it later.

Punctuate: Acids activate the salivary glands, enhancing taste sensation. If a dish is too mild, try adding a splash of vinegar or citrus when finishing.

Milder

Fresh name

Pimiento or Tomato

Poblano

Chilaca

Mirasol

Jalapeño

Dry name

Paprika

Mulato (not ripened)
Ancho (ripened first)

Pasilla

Guajillo

Chipotle (smoked)

Hotter

A pepper's name often changes when dried.

Drying intensifies flavor.

Fresh herbs may contain 80% water. When dried, most become two to three times more potent, although they lose flavor over time. Oregano, sage, rosemary, and thyme tend to retain the most flavor when dried, and work best in long-cooking dishes. Some delicate herbs, such as basil, chives, and tarragon, lose flavor when dried and are best used fresh and when added at the end of cooking.

Some fresh peppers get hotter with drying, although the bigger change is in their flavor. Avoid substituting dried peppers when a recipe calls for fresh, unless you are sure they are equivalent.

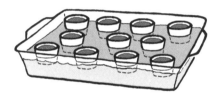

53

Bain marie

Manage moisture.

Don't crowd a pan. In ordinary circumstances, it is impossible for the temperature of water to exceed 212°F/100°C. If you cook wet food or crowd a pan, water will build up and the cooking temperature will be reduced. Use dry food and a pan size and shape that allow prompt evaporation.

Give it a bath. For cheesecakes, custards, puddings, and other fragile egg-based dishes, place the baking pan in a water bath. The oven temperature will fluctuate, but the *bain marie* will stay at 212°F/100°C, promoting even cooking and preventing curdling.

Steam your oven. While preheating, place a broiler pan beneath where bread will bake. Just after putting the bread in, carefully pour a cup of water into it. The steam will draw sugars to the bread's surface, where they will caramelize and prompt a crisp crust.

Sweat (render) your vegetables. To keep moist vegetables, such as onions, carrots, and celery, from oversaturating a dish, first gently cook them for about 5 minutes in a lightly oiled pan without browning. They will release much of their moisture as steam.

54

Menu types

Static: offers the same dishes daily for an extended time. Common at chain and fast-food restaurants. May be combined with daily specials, and may change seasonally.

Cycle: changes daily (a Monday menu, Tuesday menu, etc.) and repeats every week. Common in institutions (schools, hospitals, penitentiaries, etc.).

Market: based daily on what is currently available for purchase by the restaurant, suggesting extensive use of fresh products and seasonal variation.

Farm to table: focuses on fresh, local/regional (usually 100 miles or less), sustainable, and often organic ingredients. May change daily according to available foods.

À la carte: each item is priced and ordered separately. In a semi à la carte menu, some entrées come with a salad or side item.

Prix fixe (PREE fix, meaning "fixed price"): offers a set number of courses for a set price, with limited choices within each course. Some restaurants switch to an inexpensive prix fixe on Mondays to draw customers and repurpose leftovers. Others use a prix fixe menu on busy holidays, such as Mother's Day, to simplify kitchen operations.

55

- [ ] Name of dish
- [ ] Total yield, individual portion size, and total portions
- [ ] List of ingredients, with exact amount of each
- [ ] Special equipment, if any
- [ ] Special *mise en place* procedures
- [ ] Step-by-step directions, including preparation time, cooking time, and temperatures
- [ ] Plating: type of plate, amount per serving, side dishes, how arranged, garnish, etc.
- [ ] Recommended wine pairing
- [ ] Storage and repurposing of leftover components

Recipe checklist

If it's too difficult to write the recipe, don't put it on the menu.

When writing a recipe for a new dish, include ingredients, equipment, methods, temperature, time, yield, garnish, plating, presentation, wine recommendation, and storage and reuse of leftovers. Before putting a new recipe on the menu, check the quality and price of all ingredients with suppliers and verify their availability for the menu's duration. The right ingredients may be a compromise among these factors.

Make sure staff cooks can follow the new recipe. Verify quality consistency, share the dishes with all involved in food service, and solicit feedback.

56

Expensive

GRAMERCY TAVERN

Nº 9 PARK

Spago

Chez Panisse

RUTH'S CHRIS STEAK HOUSE

BENIHANA

Applebee's

P.F. Chang's

Panera

Chipotle MEXICAN GRILL

Johnny Rocket's

local diner

hot dog stand

sub shop

food truck

taco stand

Chinese takeout

Inexpensive

Conventional menu

Exotic (foreign, avant-garde) menu

Remember why guests walk through the door.

Guests seek more from a dining experience than to satisfy their appetites: comfort, prestige, value, relaxation, artistry, social fun, or perhaps just a good place to watch the game.

Be clear why customers choose your restaurant. Prioritize what they most need. If they visit for value, create an impression of abundance on the plate and refill water glasses, coffee cups, and bread baskets without waiting for guests to ask. If they seek artistry, take the extra step in plating. If they desire a family atmosphere, have plenty of kid-sized choices on the menu and take spills and tantrums in stride.

When catering, be likewise guest-centric. Be sure to understand the occasion, level of formality/informality, venue, and general age range of guests. However, in all cases, be wary of mission creep. It's almost always best to do fewer things, better, than to try to make something for everyone.

57

Quick fixes for kitchen problems

Shortage of fresh vegetables: Frozen peas and canned corn are almost always of good quality, and are worthy substitutes for fresh as long as they are not featured.

Shortage of fresh herbs: Use their dried counterparts where they will be less evident, such as in sauces, and save the fresh ones for finishing and presentation.

Lobster dies just before cooking: Cook it anyway. If the meat is firm and smells fresh, use for lobster bisque or soufflé and save the shells for stock. If mushy, discard.

Broken Hollandaise sauce: Restart with a fresh yolk, and whisk tho broken sauce into it.

Out of wine: For white wine, try substituting one or a combination of: apple juice, white vermouth, chicken stock, vinegar (rice, apple cider), white grape juice, and diluted lemon juice. For red wine, try balsamic vinegar, red vermouth, beef stock, red grape juice, red wine vinegar, and apple cider vinegar.

58

Keep guests informed.

Customers will usually accept mistakes—and might consider them part of the fun of the dining experience—if they feel their needs have been understood and respected.

Be open about errors and oversights. If understaffed, let guests know, and provide plenty of bread and water while they wait for service. If a dish is running late, inform the guest immediately. If a customer points out an error in food delivered to the table, acknowledge the mistake. And unless leaving the incorrect food would be offensive, don't take it away until the replacement is delivered, as a diner may be uncomfortable having an empty setting while their companions eat.

59

Serve a just-enough portion.

In fine dining, when portioning an entrée or dessert, use your hand (assuming it is of average size) as a rough guide. Your palm approximates how much protein or starch to plate. Two or three fingers approximate the amount of vegetable, such as green beans or asparagus, to serve.

A too-large serving risks suggesting that the food was cheap and hastily prepared. A just-enough portion conveys that care and quality were elevated over quantity, and that guests should eat more slowly to savor and enjoy. Too, a just-enough portion leaves room for guests to enjoy appetizers, desserts, and other menu items.

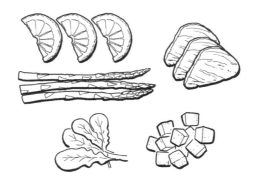

60

Be a geometer.

Because food comes from nature, one may be inclined to randomize its presentation to make it look "natural." But a plate that uses strong geometries will almost always look more appealing than one arranged indiscriminately.

Counterpoint food shapes, sizes, and textures so that each food makes the others more unique. In a stir-fry, for example, try matchstick carrots, diced onions, half-round mushrooms, and long, curly pepper slices.

Cut foods precisely. Make the fiftieth dice look like the first one.

Anticipate how foods will look on the diner's fork or spoon. Do you want three items on every salad forkful? Four colors in every soup spoonful? What proportions and sizes of ingredients will produce the desired effect?

Make a strong move on the plate. If a plate is unavoidably random, make *one* strong move to convey intention. A long green vegetable or neatly shingled proteins can organize an otherwise messy plate.

A salad may be arranged loosely, but don't be disorganized. Strategically place finishing items, such as croutons, cherry tomatoes, micro-greens, and crumbled cheese, to suggest layers of discovery.

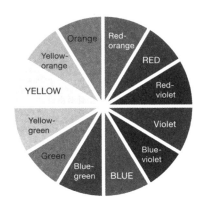

61

Nine more ways to make a plate look better

1   **Design the negative space.** Create a wide border around a centered presentation, or arrange food asymmetrically to draw the eye to it.

2   **Create visual depth.** Arrange or shingle foods at different heights, but make sure they will stay put when carried to the dining room.

3   **Bed it.** Place the feature or entire presentation on a bed of greens, pasta, or grains.

4   **Use white plates.** Colored plates overwhelm most (but not all) food. Even when staying with white, explore textures and finishes that complement and celebrate the food—for example, irregular earthenware for an organic menu.

5   **Vary plate shapes.** If round is too predictable, try square, triangular, and oval, keeping an eye on the creation of negative space.

6   **Use complementary colors.** Combine colors that are roughly opposite on the color wheel for visual balance. Place bright, fresh greens—even snippings of celery leaves—atop a dark brown dish to offset and enliven it.

7   **Use a contrasting garnish.** Don't make it superfluous; a garnish should be eaten.

8   **Paint the sauce.** Paint a stroke with a pastry brush, medicine-drop accent dots, or ladle a ring of color in the plate's negative space.

9   **Dust the perimeter of the plate with green herbs or black pepper** if the food colors are too sedate or monochromatic.

62

The power of five

Five ingredients per dish: You can use more, but if struggling to create a successful dish, you may be doing too much—often, combining too many flavors. Try using fewer ingredients, which may allow you to purchase *better* ingredients and waste less. Simple food made from the best ingredients is almost always the best food.

Five components on a plate: A plate will look crowded and overambitious if it contains more than five components: feature, complement, side, counterpoint, and garnish.

Five choices per menu category: In better restaurants, it's usually best to limit choices within menu categories (e.g., appetizers, main courses, pastas) to about five. Seven is the maximum; more than this has been shown in formal studies to delay and frustrate decision-making. Too, diners may become confused over the mission of the restaurant and question whether it can control quality over an unusually broad range.

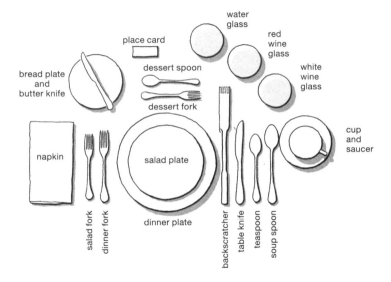

water glass

place card

red wine glass

dessert spoon

white wine glass

bread plate and butter knife

dessert fork

cup and saucer

napkin

salad plate

salad fork

dinner fork

dinner plate

backscratcher

table knife

teaspoon

soup spoon

Traditional formal place setting

Visual surprise heightens emotional response.

The traditional American dinner features a protein (meat or fish), starch, vegetable, and garnish. Modern cuisine plays with this standard, which prompts the diner to approach food more slowly and thoughtfully and tune into subtleties of smell, taste, and texture. The traditional starch is pureed and presented as a bed for the protein. The vegetable is distributed around the plate to garnish other foods. Entrée components are neatly aligned on a rectangular plate, compelling the diner to consciously combine them.

Surprise elicits an emotional-aesthetic reaction, but don't provoke without purpose. A "deconstructed sandwich" that is merely a salad with a side of bread will seem silly. A vertical presentation that does not convey anything essential about the food, and that must be immediately undone by the guest, will seem pretentious. Instead, start with *why*: create presentations that respond to and comment on the context—the restaurant theme or setting, or the nature and origin of the food itself.

"People don't buy what you do, they buy why you do it."

—SIMON SINEK

65

Feeding the crowd

Maximize buffet access. A wall might seem an appealing location for a buffet table in order to leave the room open for socializing, but this will cause severe congestion at the buffet—and may even foster competitiveness. Whenever possible, allow access from all sides, even if the buffet is in the middle of the room. Consider having separate, well-spaced tables for cold foods, hot foods, beverages, and desserts.

Put the inexpensive stuff first. In buffets, place bread and salads where they will be encountered before the main dishes. This matches the order in which most guests will eat, and discourages them from piling on expensive foods that they may not finish.

Scatter the food to foster mingling. For social events featuring small plates or hors d'oeuvres, small service tables spaced around a large room, each featuring a different food, will prompt movement and increase social interactions.

66

A few hot hors d'oeuvres can warm a whole room. Cold foods make catering easier, but always try to serve one or two hot foods. Each round brought into the room will feel to guests like a mini-event within the larger event.

Watch faces. Social events can prompt anxiety and confusion. Guests' faces will often subconsciously express what they need to be comfortable.

Stay vegetarian-ready.

In anticipation of vegetarian customers, keep animal products separate from vegetables when performing *mise en place*. And regardless of what appears on the menu, be ready to alter several menu items, have several vegetarian recipes at the ready, and keep fallbacks on hand. A number of frozen vegetables are agreeable, including peas, corn, pearl onions, and spinach. Canned corn, artichokes, and water chestnuts can also work well, especially when combined in a tofu- or rice-based entrée. Butternut squash will last a long time, making it good to keep around for the unexpected.

If a vegetarian dish seems lackluster, bolster it with umami-rich vegetarian ingredients, such as shitake mushrooms, ripe tomatoes, spinach, and high-quality soy sauce.

67

Keeping kosher

Kosher food meets kashrut, the Jewish dietary law set forth in the Torah. In general, the following apply:

- **Meat, poultry, and fish:** Mammals that are split-hoofed and chew their cud, including antelope, bison, cow, deer, goat, and sheep, are permitted. Twenty-four species of bird are forbidden; those allowed include chicken, duck, goose, and turkey. Fish must have fins and readily visible scales that can be removed easily. Shellfish are prohibited. Animal blood may not be consumed, and by-products of non-kosher animals, such as eggs, are forbidden.

- **Slaughter of animals** must minimize pain and cause instantaneous death. A slain animal must be inspected for physical abnormalities, and some blood vessels, nerves, and fat must be removed.

- **Animal and dairy products** may not be prepared with the same pots, dishes, or utensils, and may not be eaten together.

- **Nuts, grains, fruits, and vegetables** are naturally kosher, but may contain insects or insecticides or have been handled in ways that make them non-kosher. Processing and/or preparation of such foods, as well as bread, oil, wine, and condiments, require rabbinic supervision.

68

Keeping halal

Halal means "permissible." The Qur'an allows Muslims to eat what is "pure, clean, nourishing, and pleasing," and prohibits the following:

- an animal that was improperly slaughtered or already dead (i.e., not killed for food)
- an animal not killed in the name of Allah (God)
- carnivorous animals, birds of prey, and land animals without external ears
- blood
- swlne (pork)
- intoxicating drinks
- meat from which wild animals have eaten
- meat of an animal that has been sacrificed to idols

69

Hindu food practices

Hindus believe in the interconnection of mind, body, and spirit, and that food choice affects all three.

Tamasic foods are deemed to benefit neither mind nor body and to produce anger, greed, and other negative emotions. They include meat, onions, alcohol, and spoiled, fermented, overripe, or otherwise impure foods.

Rajasic foods are believed to benefit the body, but can produce a restless or overstimulated mind. They include very hot, spicy, salty, bitter, and sour foods, as well as chocolate, coffee, tea, eggs, peppers, pickles, and processed foods.

Sattvic foods are held to be balancing to the body, purifying to the mind, and calming to the spirit. The most desirable category of food, it includes grains, nuts, fruits, vegetables, milk, clarified butter, and cheese.

70

Pork is prohibited, as are cows, which are considered sacred.

"The opportunity here in the U.S. is so unique. . . . Christians, Jews, Hindus, Muslims and Buddhists, all with their own connections to the spiritual aspects of food and with lessons that we can learn from each other."

— MARCUS SAMUELSSON

71

If you aren't comfortable on a farm, you won't be comfortable in a kitchen.

Success in the kitchen requires familiarity not only with food, but with food sources—the field, farm, and slaughterhouse. The atmosphere of these places differs markedly from the stainless steel expanse of the kitchen. The people are different. Clothing and shoes are different. Familiar foods look different, dirty, even bloody. But you must walk the field enough to recognize and evaluate foods in their growing state. And unless you intend to work in a vegetarian setting, you must be accepting of the slaughter of animals, while offering deep respect for the gifts they provide us.

72

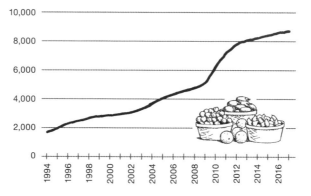

10,000
8,000
6,000
4,000
2,000
0

1994 1996 1998 2000 2002 2004 2006 2008 2010 2012 2014 2016

Farmers market directory listings in U.S., 1994–2017
Source: USDA Agricultural Marketing Service

How to shop at a farmers market

Arrive early for the best selection. Arrive late for the best values.

Buy on the second pass. Make at least one initial pass among all vendors to check quality and flavor, ask questions, make notes, and menu-plan.

Bargain. Ask vendors politely, "How much if I take five pounds of each?" "What will you take for the remainder of the lug?"

Develop relationships with trusted vendors. Return to them often. See if you can buy directly from them, outside the farmers market.

73

Herbs	**Spices**
from the leafy, green parts of plants	from non-leafy plant parts (stem, bark, seeds, root, or bulb)
used fresh or dried	usually dried
usually grown in temperate zones	usually grown in tropical zones
may have medicinal or cosmetic value	may have value as preservatives or anti-inflammatory/anti-fungal agents
Examples: basil, oregano, thyme, rosemary, **parsley**, and mint	Examples: **cinnamon**, ginger, chili, clove, mustard seed

Spices were once used as money.

Spices and other flavorings were so valuable in the Fertile Crescent and other early settlement regions that they were used for trade or barter. In the Roman Empire, workers were often paid in *sal* (meaning salt, actually a mineral), hence our word *salary*. And when the Visigoths attacked Rome in 408 CE, they demanded 3,000 pounds of pepper as part of the city's ransom.

In 14th-century Europe, saffron counterfeiters became such a problem that the Safranschou code was enacted, under which saffron defrauders were thrown in prison and even executed. Genuine saffron today can cost $1,500 per pound.

74

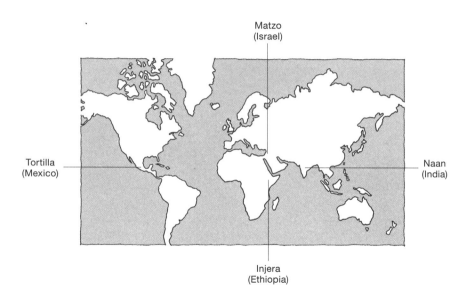

Present-day flatbreads

Hunter-gatherers liked flatbreads.

Crude flatbreads were first developed around 10,000 BCE. By 3,000 BCE, Egyptians were making leavened (raised by yeast) breads. Ancient flatbreads were made by mixing wild wheats such as einkorn and emmer with water, and baking the mixture in a brick or clay oven that could be heated as high as 480°F (249°C). Flatbreads today use a similar recipe of flour or whole grains mixed with water and salt.

75

Arabica

large, oval bean with wavy crease

temperamental grower; small trees are easy to harvest but are susceptible to pests, disease, poor climate

Robusta

small bean with straight crease

robust grower; high caffeine content protects the plant, but poor growing conditions may yield a rubbery taste

Goats discovered coffee.

Coffee, by one account, is said to have been first consumed by humans in the 9th century, after an Ethiopian herder noticed his goats had become agitated from eating coffee berries.

Two coffee species are dominant today. **Arabica,** with a nuanced flavor, bright body, and pleasing acidity, accounts for two-thirds or more of the world's production. **Robusta,** with strong, chocolatey notes, heavy body, and low acidity, accounts for about one-quarter. Arabica is widely considered superior; sophisticated drinkers may find Robusta burnt- or grainy-tasting. However, Robusta is good for espresso, as it has almost twice the caffeine of Arabica. It can add a "bass note" to an Arabica brew, and it might please those who like a "muddy cup" with lots of cream and sugar.

It is feared that 60% of the world's 124 wild coffee species, including Arabica, will go extinct in the next 60 years due to climate change and habitat destruction.

Selected white wines

generally lighter → generally fuller

Muscadet	Extra dry, crisp, minerally, acidic
Riesling	Dry to sweet, acidic
Sauvignon Blanc	Dry, acidic, bright, crisp
Pinot Grigio, Pinot Gris Dry	Medium acidic, zesty
Viognier	Dry but fruity; low acidity
California Chardonnay	Semi-dry, rich, oaky or buttery

Selected red wines

generally lighter → generally fuller

Rosé	Varies depending on origin
Beaujolais Nouveau	Young wine; light body
Pinot Noir	Acidic, fragrant
Rioja, Tempranillo	Dry, medium tannins
Syrah	Peppery finish
Merlot	Dry but fruit-forward
Cabernet Sauvignon	Long finish, deep fruit, bold tannins

Reading a wine label

Varietal: The type of grape used, e.g., Merlot, Pinot Grigio. If named on a U.S.-sold wine, at least 75% of contents must be that varietal. If a wine is labeled a **blend** or **table wine,** it contains several types of grapes, which might not be from the named vineyard. Table wines tend to work better as a meal accompaniment than as featured wines.

Country of origin: In the U.S., must be on the label. **Old World** wines are from the oldest wine regions (Europe, parts of the Middle East), very old vine stock, and mostly cooler climates. They are usually refined in taste, light-bodied, and lower in alcohol. **New World** wines, generally from warmer climates, tend to be fruitier, bolder, and fuller-bodied.

Estate bottled: If labeled as such, the wine must have been grown, produced, and bottled on the vineyard indicated on the label.

Reserve: No official meaning in the U.S.

Alcohol by volume (ABV): Ranges from about 7% to 24%; higher indicates a riper grape. Must be indicated on label if over 14%.

Sulfites: All wines have some natural sulfites. In the U.S., the label must say "contains sulfites" when over 10 ppm (parts per million).

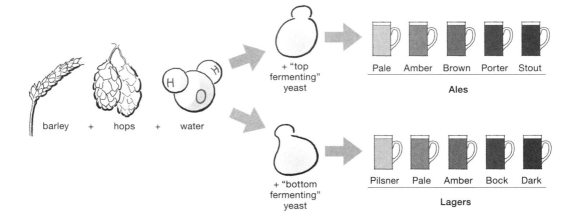

barley + hops + water

+ "top fermenting" yeast

Pale Amber Brown Porter Stout

Ales

+ "bottom fermenting" yeast

Pilsner Pale Amber Bock Dark

Lagers

A beer is an ale or a lager.

Beers are confusing because there are so many, and more are created every day. Even traditional beers can confuse, in part because beer makers aren't always rigorous with terminology: some will call a lighter brew a pilsner and a darker one a lager, for example, but a pilsner is actually a *type* of lager.

The basics of beer are simple: it is made from water, malted (partially germinated) barley, hops (a semi-bitter flower that balances barley's sweetness), and yeast. A different grain is sometimes used in lieu of barley, as in wheat beer and rye beer.

The difference between ales and lagers lies in the yeast: ales use a "top fermenting" strain that activates at about 60 to 75°F (15 to 24°C), while lagers use a "bottom fermenting" variety that activates at about 40 to 58°F (4 to 14°C).

Beer preferences are highly personal, but in general, ales are sweeter and fruitier than lagers. Light beers tend to go better with lighter dishes, dark beers with heartier meals. A hoppy beer can intensify a spicy dish or cut through a fatty meal.

78

Worcestershire sauce
anchovies, sardines

Barbecue sauce
pecans

Sweet-and-sour sauce
wheat, soy

Canned tuna
casein, soy protein

Allergens often found in familiar foods

If you're allergic to dust, you might be allergic to shellfish.

Ordinary house dust mites belong to *Arthropoda*, the same phylum as crabs, lobsters, shrimp, and other shellfish. Studies indicate that sensitivity to dust mites is a reaction to tropomyosins, a protein in arthropods that facilitates their muscle movement.

About 4% of people have a food allergy of some kind. The most common in adults are peanuts, shellfish, fish, tree nuts, and eggs. If a dish contains allergens, indicate it on the menu, e.g., pecan-encrusted trout. Contamination can occur indirectly, via trace amounts on hands/gloves, utensils, pans, and serving trays, so make the dish again if anything, even a garnish, is suspected to have come in contact with an allergen. Deliver nonallergenic dishes to the table separately from the others.

Don't eat raw beans.

Raw beans contain lectin, a deadly poison. Its concentration is highest in kidney beans. Before cooking beans, soak them overnight. Discard the water, rinse them thoroughly, and boil in fresh water until fork tender. Failure to cook adequately at a high enough temperature may actually increase harmful compounds. Other food poisons include:

Potatoes are a member of the deadly nightshade family. Their leaves, stems, and green spots on the skin contain a glycoalkaloid poison. Death is rare.

Cherry, plum, apricot, and peach pits contain compounds that can produce cyanide when crushed and digested.

Tapioca is from the fruit of the cassava plant, the leaves of which contain cyanide.

Rhubarb leaves house toxic oxalic acid. Stems and roots are safe.

Bitter almonds contain cyanide before processing; a handful can kill an adult. Almonds sold in the U.S. are heat-treated to remove the poison.

Castor beans: although 4 to 8 will kill an adult, castor bean oil is a common health supplement and is sometimes added to candies, chocolate, and other foods.

Fugu (FOO-goo), a pufferfish, is a delicacy in Asia. Its organs contain tetrodotoxin, a lethal poison, which by law must be removed before sale.

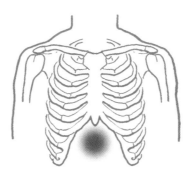

Heimlich pressure point

Kitchen aid

Cuts: If edges are ragged, tissue is exposed, or blood pulses or spurts, call 911. If anything is severed, wrap in clean plastic, gauze, or cloth and place on ice. Press a clean cloth to wound, elevate at least 15 minutes without checking. When bleeding stops, rinse gently with water. Ice can reduce swelling.

Burns: Place under cool running water for 15 minutes. No ointments, butter, or ice. If the burn blisters, turns white, or is bigger than your hand, call 911. Do not break blisters or remove any stuck fabric. Separate burned fingers, cover with a clean bandage. Elevate above the heart. Prevent shock by elevating feet.

Allergic reactions: Call 911. If victim carries an Epi-Pen, plunge into thigh and hold for at least 5 seconds. Massage injection site to help absorption. If possible, have victim take an antihistamine, lie down with feet elevated, and loosen belts and tight clothing.

Choking: Call 911. From there, experts do not agree on the ideal response. If the victim is making noise, they are breathing and might cough up the obstruction. If quiet, either back blows or the Heimlich maneuver may work.

Chemicals in the eyes: Immediately flush with running water for 15 minutes. If contact lenses are still in after flush, take them out. Call 911.

81

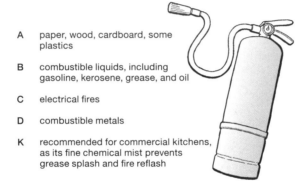

A	paper, wood, cardboard, some plastics
B	combustible liquids, including gasoline, kerosene, grease, and oil
C	electrical fires
D	combustible metals
K	recommended for commercial kitchens, as its fine chemical mist prevents grease splash and fire reflash

Fire extinguisher classes

Don't pour water on a grease fire.

If a fire occurs in a stovetop pan, it usually can be smothered with a pan lid. Salt or baking soda also can be used to smother, but a lot is required. The best method is a dry chemical fire extinguisher. Blanket the fire with the fine spray mist. Clean up thoroughly afterward, as the chemicals will contaminate the kitchen.

Never pour water on a grease fire, as this will spatter the burning grease and increase the possibility of injury. And never carry a burning vessel to a "safer" place, as this will increase the chances of spreading the fire.

Chill.

Cookies: Put cookie dough in the freezer for 30 minutes before baking. This will prevent the fat, once the dough is placed in the oven, from melting before the other ingredients, resulting in a deliciously thick cookie instead of a flat-all-over cookie.

Pastry dough: Warm butter blends too readily with flour, resulting in a uniformly dense dough. Freezing small butter pieces for 20 to 30 minutes before adding them to the flour will keep them cold and separate, producing buttery pockets and a flaky crust.

Raw beef is easier to slice thin if placed in the freezer for 30 to 60 minutes. This can be helpful for stir-fry dishes and carpaccio, an appetizer of very thin, lightly seasoned, raw beef. Bacon is also easier to slice if put in a freezer for 15 to 20 minutes.

Oysters and other shellfish are easier to open when chilled: 10 to 15 minutes in a freezer will relax the seal.

Baked lasagna: Thoroughly refrigerating the entire pan after par-baking will allow it to be cut into attractive "bricks" for final cooking and plating.

83

Fake kitchen facts

1   The seeds are the hottest part of a chile. (Truth: it's the fleshy, white ribs.)

2   Alcohol burns off in cooking. (Truth: it only partly dissipates.)

3   Use a sunny windowsill to ripen tomatoes. (Truth: a warm, dark place is best.)

4   Add oil to pasta water to prevent clumping. (Truth: most oil will remain on the surface. To prevent sticking, use a large pot and keep the pasta moving.)

5   Wood cutting boards harbor bacteria. (Truth: internal bacteria tend to die quickly.)

6   Flip meats only once. (Truth: turning often can produce a satisfactory result.)

7   Lard is unhealthy. (Truth: Lard is lower in saturated fat and cholesterol than butter.)

8   Sear meat to seal in juices. (Truth: searing does not create a moisture-tight barrier.)

9   Don't freeze thawed meat. (Truth: it will be no less safe if handled properly.)

10   Baby carrots are baby carrots. (Truth: they are trimmed from mature carrots.)

84

Use one spoon for cooking and separate spoons for tasting.

Ten mistakes of the inexperienced cook

1 Improper or inadequate *mise en place*

2 Poor timing, resulting in foods not being completed in the proper sequence

3 Not reading or knowing a recipe before starting

4 A not hot-enough pan, particularly in preparing proteins

5 Using the wrong cut of meat for the dish or cooking method

6 Overcrowding a pan when sautéing or baking

7 Cooking starches in a too-small pot, resulting in clumping

8 Overcooking due to not allowing for carryover cooking, or because of a fear of serving undercooked food

9 Not using enough salt or not salting at the proper time

10 Not tasting a dish before serving it

85

toque (hat): catches sweat and loose hairs; height allows air movement above head. In fine dining, indicates a chef is classically trained; elsewhere, may be a ball cap or bandanna.

double-breasted jacket: white repels heat, projects cleanliness

apron: helps prevent burns; can be quickly removed

pants: dark or houndstooth

hand towel: worn around back, on belt

protective shoes: comfortable for standing; nonslip soles and steel or plastic toe caps

Standard chef's uniform

Why the chef's jacket is double-breasted

The front of a chef's jacket is reversible; it can go left over right or right over left. This allows a chef, when entering the dining room to greet guests, to rebutton it and feature the clean side.

Additionally, the jacket is made from a double layer of heavy cotton or cotton-poly, usually fire resistant, to protect against hot spills and splatters. Cloth toggles or buttons are used instead of plastic ones, which can break or melt into food. The vented cuffs turn up, getting them out of the way of food and leaving a fresh side for show.

Restaurant / retail
indie and chain, food trucks,
food stores and courts

**Institutional /
corporate**
food service in
colleges, hos-
pitals, nursing
homes, corpo-
rate offices

Catering / private chef
special events as well as
regular service in private
homes

Commercial / industrial / wholesale
producers, suppliers, and vendors
serving restaurants and retail venues

Media / influencer
food styling, marketing, recipe test-
ing, sales, writing and criticism

Culinary careers

School teaches you how to cook.
Experience teaches you how to be a chef.

All chefs are cooks, but not all cooks are chefs. A cook does the everyday *mise en place* for a station or an entire kitchen but may work on only one station. A chef oversees the cooks and knows how to expertly work all stations. Cooks are usually paid hourly, while a chef is salaried. A cook may prepare a dish delivered to the dining room, but the chef's name and reputation are attached to it.

A cook has learned specific skills, employs them in consistent ways, and usually follows a recipe. A chef also has many specific skills, but can intuitively modify a recipe to achieve a desired outcome. A cook may know how to make all foods; a chef knows which foods complement others. A chef cooks from the head and the heart, and knows that an understanding of ingredients and technique trumps any recipe. A cook knows how; a chef knows why.

87

"You have no choice as a professional chef: you have to repeat, repeat, repeat, repeat until it becomes part of yourself. I certainly don't cook the same way I did 40 years ago, but the technique remains. And that's what the student needs to learn: the technique."

—JACQUES PÉPIN

88

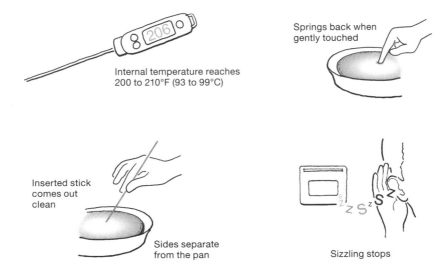

Internal temperature reaches
200 to 210°F (93 to 99°C)

Springs back when
gently touched

Inserted stick
comes out
clean

Sides separate
from the pan

Sizzling stops

Signs a cake is done baking

Be present.

The primary kitchen senses may be sight, smell, taste, and touch, but listening will also keep you in touch with food and help you gauge your cooking progress. There's no need to watch water heat; it will tick increasingly as it warms, "rumble" as it approaches boiling, and ultimately yield to a tenor of bubbles rapidly breaking the surface. A boiling sauce sounds different from a simmering sauce, and one can hear a sauce left to simmer grow thicker. A food should sizzle when placed in a pan; if it doesn't, take it out and keep heating the pan.

A ticking oven is cooling; a whoosh means it is heating. A baking cake may hiss and tick, while a fully baked cake is quiet. Fully baked bread sounds rich and a little hollow when tapped; a finished pie will burble.

A fresh vegetable will snap. A ripe melon will sound full, yet a little hollow, when tapped, while an unripe melon will offer a mild thud.

Repurpose rather than reuse.

Menu-plan for multiple uses. Have multiple menu uses for every food item. This way, if one dish goes unordered, the food will be consumed in another.

Never serve the same dish left over. When you put a cooked item back into the cooler, it should be to repurpose it the next day, not to serve it as the same dish—no matter how fresh and flavorful it remains. Use leftover rice to make fried rice; turn leftover risotto into croquettes; shred leftover chicken for soup or chicken salad; and reuse cooked steak in fajitas, pot pies, and stews. Use day-old bread for bread crumbs, stuffing, pudding, and croutons.

Repurpose preparation scraps. Systematize kitchen operations so every scrap created by primary preparation is immediately repurposed. Use carcasses and bones in stocks, and extra meat and fish pieces in soups, stews, chowders, meatloaf, meatballs, amuse-bouches (ah-MOOZ-boosh-ez, literally "mouth amusers," small gifts from the chef), and charcuterie (cold prepared meats). Render animal fat for use as a cooking fat. Use vegetable scraps and stems from chopped herbs to flavor stocks and purees.

cooled and ready-to-eat foods
(cheese, deli meat)

vegetables and fruit

fish

solid pork and beef

fish and ground meat

whole and ground poultry

floor

Cooler shelf storage order

Food storage

Containers: Use airtight containers made of BPA-free plastic or polycarbonate, glass, or stainless steel. Label each with the contents and the date purchased or stored.

Organize by category, and in a way that makes it easy to find things when busy. In the storeroom and refrigerator, label shelves as well as foods; when a shelf goes empty, the label will tell you what to buy. Post a map of the room on the door.

Store meat on the lowest shelf so juices don't contaminate foods below. However, check codes, which typically require that all food be stored 6" or more above the floor.

Don't overload the cooler, as this may overwork the cooling equipment and create inconsistent temperatures.

Dry foods: Store in a dark space under 70°F/21°C, and if possible closer to 50°F/10°C. Use a dehumidifier if conditions warrant.

First in, first out (FIFO): Store new food behind old so the older food is used first.

EPA hierarchy for reducing food waste

Ten ways to run a greener kitchen

1   Cultivate relationships with local farmers and suppliers. Minimize the use of foods that are locally out of season.

2   Buy certified organic fish, and meats/poultry that are hormone- and antibiotic-free, free range, and vegetarian fed.

3   Grow herbs and vegetables outside, on the roof, or in an indoor cultivator.

4   Maintain a composting pile, hire a composting service, or partner with a local farm that will use food waste for animal feed.

5   Install a plumbing system that recycles gray water and runoff from the roof and site. In restrooms, use waterless urinals and touchless sink sensors.

6   Buy used furnishings or ones made from recycled or renewable materials.

7   Sell unsold prepared foods, such as desserts and ready-to-go sandwiches, at reduced prices at the end of the day, or provide to employees to take home.

8   Repurpose leftovers for a family (staff) meal and/or donate to food banks and homeless shelters where permitted.

9   Recycle old cooking oil for use as biofuel.

10 Recycle plastic, glass, paper, metal, and foam products. Use 100% recyclable take-out containers, plates, and utensils, paper drinking straws, and reusable hand towels and napkins.

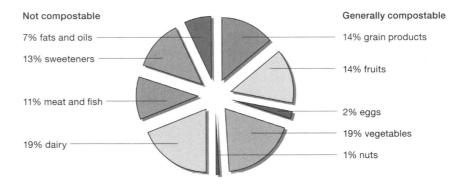

Not compostable

7% fats and oils

13% sweeteners

11% meat and fish

19% dairy

Generally compostable

14% grain products

14% fruits

2% eggs

19% vegetables

1% nuts

U.S. food waste by food category

How to compost

1   Choose a location with good sun exposure to best activate microbes. Smell is not an issue in a proper compost. If concerned about appearance, use an enclosed, waist-high container about 3 feet across. Otherwise, an open outdoor space will suffice, but protect it from animals with a barrier.

2   Add plant-based waste only. Include **brown waste** (paper, wood, straw, and leaves) and **green waste** (fruits, vegetables, lawn clippings, and coffee grounds) in a ratio of about 3 to 1. Brown waste is rich in carbon, which feeds the microorganisms that break down the scraps. Green waste supplies nitrogen, which will help build the new soil. Don't compost oils, diseased plants, or animal products (meat, dairy, fats, pet waste). Break apart large items to speed decomposition. Add some previously composted material to boost microorganism population.

3   Keep the pile slightly moist. Turn it over and loosen each week for aeration. With the right mix of air and moisture, it will smell earthy, not stinky.

4   If progress after a few weeks is slow, add more green material. If it's smelly, add more brown material, turn the pile more frequently, and reduce moisture.

5   The compost is ready when it acquires the appearance and texture of rich brown soil. Add it to your garden soil a few times a year.

A $2 chicken can cost $2 million.

Poultry is responsible for about 25% of food-related illnesses, more than any other food. Restaurants, according to a comprehensive study, were the most common source. The most oft-cited factors were improper handling and inadequate cooking. Liabilities for restaurants also include:

Biological hazards: microorganisms including bacteria, molds, yeasts, viruses, fungi, staph, botulism, salmonella, strep, *E. coli*, and listeria

Chemical hazards: cleaning agents, pesticides, and other toxic liquids

Physical hazards in food, such as particles of glass, plastic, metal, wood, dust, and paint

Property hazards: slippery floors; icy, poorly lit, and dangerous sidewalks and parking lots; and dangers from buildings, fences, trees, and utility poles. Restaurants may be liable for the safety of cars, delivery trucks, and customer property.

Drinking hazards: A restaurant may be legally liable for serving too many drinks to a customer.

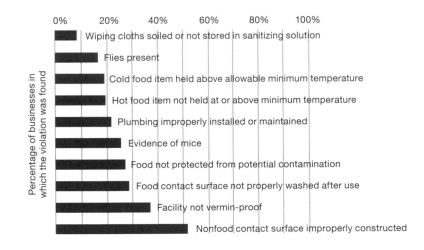

0%   20%   40%   60%   80%   100%

Percentage of businesses in which the violation was found

Wiping cloths soiled or not stored in sanitizing solution

Flies present

Cold food item held above allowable minimum temperature

Hot food item not held at or above minimum temperature

Plumbing improperly installed or maintained

Evidence of mice

Food not protected from potential contamination

Food contact surface not properly washed after use

Facility not vermin-proof

Nonfood contact surface improperly constructed

Most common food service violations in New York City
Source: NYC Open Data via ConsumerProtect.com

A surface must be cleaned before it can be sanitized.

Cleaning is the removal, without germicides, of unwanted soil from surfaces that have a low risk of transferring pathogens to foods, such as floors and windows.

Sanitizing is required by health codes for food contact surfaces. Sanitizing reduces the number of microorganisms on a clean surface to safe levels using hot water (at least 171°F/77°C), steam, or chemicals. A product described as a sanitizer must kill more than 99% of specified bacteria. Sanitizers have no effect on viruses and fungi, however.

Disinfection should kill 100% of the organisms claimed on the product label.

Auguste Escoffier (1846–1935)

The chef is chief.

Chef is French for "chief." It was not considered an English word even a century ago. It derives from the Latin *caput*, meaning "head," a root that lives on today in *per capita* (per head) and *decapitate* (to remove the head from).

Chef became associated with the culinary world through the French use of *chef de cuisine*, "head of the kitchen." But a chef may be responsible for much more than food preparation, including anything related to the dining experience: decor, lighting, food ordering, health inspections, even plumbing. Whatever goes wrong, the chef may have to fix it.

96

How to replace a faucet

1   If there's a garbage disposal, turn off the power to it. Turn off water valves under the sink, and turn on the faucet to relieve pressure. Photograph everything for reference.

2   Disconnect the water supply lines with a wrench, using a bucket to catch any water.

3   Have a helper hold the faucet from above while you loosen and remove the nuts underneath. Remove the faucet and thoroughly clean the sink surface.

4   Place the gasket supplied with the new faucet over the holes in the sink, and set the deck plate. See manufacturer's instructions if caulk or sealant is called for.

5   Feed the faucet lines through the holes in the sink. Install washers and nuts on the underside. If you used caulk or sealant in Step 4, wipe away any excess underneath.

6   For pull-down faucets, attach the quick-connect hose to the supply pipe. Pull down on the hose and attach the weight.

7   Connect the water supply lines, being careful not to overtighten.

8   Turn on the water a little and check for leaks. Tighten connections if necessary. Let the water run full-on for a few minutes to purge air in the system.

Unusual items in a chef's toolkit

Bricks: cleaned and wrapped in foil, used to make dishes such as *pollo al mattone*, an Italian method of cooking chicken under a weight, which results in crisp skin and juicy meat in about half the normal cooking time

Dental floss: for cutting layer cakes, roll cookies, soft cheeses, dough, and cheesecake

Medicine dropper: useful for presentation, such as dotting soy or dessert sauce

Nail polish or plasticized paint: for putting identifying marks on one's tools

Ruler: to measure rise in dough, the size or thickness of steaks and other foods, and level the contents of measuring cups

Small spray bottles: for moistening pie dough, coating pans with oil, and misting salad dressing on delicate greens

Tweezers or needle-nose pliers: for removing pin bones from fish and picking out tiny bits of eggshell

How to survive when lost

Prepare. Show up early, walk around, learn where everything is. Ask other workers about each piece of equipment. Take notes on how things are done. Learn the menu.

Observe the kitchen culture. See if it is reserved or happy-go-lucky.

Check your station to verify everything is in place and every container is full. You will not have time to restock when the kitchen gets busy. When orders arrive, scan again to verify that you have everything needed.

Repeat everything the expeditor says to you to the expeditor, and say it twice more in your head. Keep talking to a minimum and focus on the orders.

Breathe. A busy period can provide an exhilarating "rush," but when things are hectic, take an occasional, brief moment to reflect on what is happening.

Take it to the cooler. If a private conversation with a coworker is needed, have someone cover your station and, if it won't suggest impropriety, use the walk-in cooler. It's nearly soundproof, and the cold will help you resolve your problem quickly.

If there's nothing to do, see if anyone, including the dishwasher, needs help.

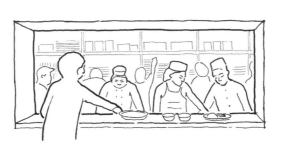

You can't escape people by going to the kitchen.

Because the kitchen is "back of the house" with little public interaction, it may seem an ideal place for introverts. But introversion is not possible within the kitchen brigade. You must be an active communicator, listen carefully and respectfully to instructions, not take personally the commands barked at you, and interact clearly and respectfully with those under you.

When personal differences seem insurmountable, remind yourself that all workers in the kitchen share a central interest: to deliver meals that are consistent in quality, taste, and appearance, and that match the chef's vision. The one hundredth meal the brigade prepares must look like it came from one hand, and was created solely for the guest who ordered it.

100

"No one who cooks, cooks alone. Even at her most solitary, a cook in the kitchen is surrounded by generations of cooks past, the advice and menus of cooks present, the wisdom of cookbook writers."

—LAURIE COLWIN (1944–1992)

101

Notes

Lesson 35: Ecotrust, "A Fresh Look at Frozen Fish: Expanding Market Opportunities for Community Fishermen," July 2017.

Lesson 76: Aaron Davis, Head of Coffee Research at the Royal Botanic Gardens, Kew, England.

Lesson 94: Chai, S. J.; Cole, D.; Nisler, A.; and Mahon, B. E. "Poultry: the most common food in outbreaks with known pathogens, United States, 1998–2012." *Epidemiology and Infection* 145, no. 2 (2017): 316–25.

Index

allergens, 79, 81
amuse-bouche, 90

backscratcher, 64
bain marie, 54
baking, 1, 41, 49, 54, 89
beans, 80
beef
    aging, 26
    cattle raising, 26
    cuts, 28
    doneness, 30
    grading, 27
    marbling, 27
    tenderizing, 29
    safe-to-eat temperature, 31
    salting/brining of, 29, 41
    storage, 91
beer, 78
blanching, 32, 41
Bourdain, Anthony, 7
braising, 1, 19, 28
bread
    flatbreads, 75
    flour selection, 48
    general, 9, 18, 23, 54
browning and/or caramelizing,
    1, 2, 3, 14, 17, 18, 19, 21,
    42, 48

buffets, 66
butter,
    in baking dough, 83
    cholesterol in, 43
    clarified, 42
    flavor/character, 23, 24
    ghee, 24, 42
    monter au buerre, 42
    salted vs. unsalted, 42
    in sauces, 38, 42
    sman, 42
    smoke point, 20
caramelizing (browning), 3, 17,
    18, 52, 54
careers in culinary field, 87, 88
Carême, Marie-Antoine
    38
carryover cooking, 31, 85
catering, 57, 66
cheese, 47
chef
    experience, 87, 88
    meaning, 87, 96
    responsibilities, 4, 96, 97
    uniform, 86
chicken/poultry
    how to fabricate, 25
    par-cooking, 32
    parts of, uses for, 25

    safe-to-eat temperature, 31
    sauces for, 38
    as source of illness, 94
    stock, 25, 36
    storage, 91
    U.S. consumption of, 29
cholesterol, 43, 84
cleaning and sanitizing, 95
coffee, 76
Colwin, Laurie, 101
composting, 93
convection oven, 33

deep-frying, 1, 19, 41
deglazing, 52
diet and nutrition, 43, 44
dried foods
    herbs and spices, 74
    peppers, 53
dry cooking, 1

eggs
    allergies, 79
    in baking, 50, 54
    cholesterol, 43
    dating and packaging, 50
    emulsifier, 40
    measuring, 49
    properties, 50

eggs (*cont'd*)
    in sauces, 38
    as thickener, 37
emulsifiers, 40
environment and
    sustainability, 92, 93
Escoffier, Auguste, 38, 96

farms and farmers markets,
    72, 73
fat(s)
    in butter, 42
    in cheese, 47
    composting of, 93
    diet and health issues, 43
    in fish, 34
    lard, 84
    marbling in beef, 27
    melting point, 14
    oils, *see* oils and fats,
        cooking
    roux, 37
    types and flavors, 23, 24
finish cooking, 32
fire, putting out, 82
first aid, 81
fish
    fat in, 34
    fresh vs. frozen, 35
    selecting, 34, 35
    shellfish, 35, 41, 68, 79,
        83
    U.S. consumption of,
        29

flavor
    defined, 51
    enhancing/focusing, 18,
        52, 53
flour, 48
food storage, 91
fresh vs. frozen food, 35,
    58, 67

garde manger, 4
ghee, 24, 42
grilling, 1, 3

Halal, 69
Heimlich maneuver, 81
herbs and spices, 53, 74
Hindu foods, 70

kitchen
    behavior in, 8, 99, 100
    brigade/chain of com-
        mand, 3, 4, 100
    communication, 8, 99, 100
    cooking stations, 4
    organization and
        operations, 4, 5, 6,
        7, 90
    plumbing, 97
    problems, 58, 59
    sounds in, 89
    terminology, 3, 4, 5
knife cuts, 12, 13
knives, 9, 10, 11
kosher foods, 41, 68

leftovers, 14, 32, 55, 56, 90, 92

Maillard reaction, 18
measurement, of ingredients,
    49
meats
    beef, 26, 27, 28, 29, 30, 31,
        83, 91
    carryover cooking, 31
    cuts, 28
    lamb, 28, 31
    pork, 28, 31
    poultry, 26, 31, 38, 68, 91,
        92, 94
    safe-to-eat temperatures,
        14, 31
    tenderizing, 29
    U.S. consumption of, 29
    veal, 28, 31
menus, 55, 56, 57, 63
menu-planning, 73, 90
mise en place, 6, 7, 85, 21
moist cooking, 1, 3, 27, 28, 46
moisture, managing, 54
Morgan, Heather, 44
myths and facts about food,
    84

Nosrat, Samin, 24

oils and fats, cooking
    butter, 23, 24
    fat(s), 23, 24
    flash point, 20

general, 19, 20, 21, 23, 24, 43, 84
ghee, 24, 42
lard, 23
in pan cooking, 19, 20
refined and unrefined oils, 23
smoke point, 20
taste/character, 23, 24

pan cooking, 1, 3, 18, 19, 20, 21, 22, 32, 52, 54, 85
pan flip, 22
par-cooking, 32
Pépin, Jacques, 88
peppers, 53, 84
plating/presentation, 60, 61, 62, 63, 64, 65
poisonous foods, 80
potatoes, 46, 80

recipes, how to write, 56
reduction of sauces, 37
restaurant
    guest experience, 59, 63, 64, 65
    health code violations, 95
    liabilities, 94
    mission/purpose, 57, 63, 64
rice, 45

roux, 37, 38

salad greens, 39
salt
    in baking, 41
    in butter, 42
    as tenderizer, 29
    types, 41
    when to add, 15, 41
Salt Fat Acid Heat (book), 24
Samuelsson, Marcus, 71
sauces, 37, 38, 52
sauté, 1, 3, 4, 12, 18, 19, 20, 21, 32, 52, 85
Sinek, Simon, 65
sous vide, 1
spices and herbs, 53, 74
stock, 36, 37, 41
storage of food, 91
substitutions, in cooking, 53, 58, 67

taste categories, 51
temperature
    boiling point, 14, 15, 16, 54
    browning, 18
    cake doneness, 89
    for caramelizing, 18
    convection ovens, 33
    deep frying, 19
    food danger zone, 14

food storage, 91
for Maillard reaction, 18
oil smoke points, 23
for pan cooking, 18, 19, 20
safe-to-eat, for meats, 14, 31
sanitizing, 95
spectrum, 14
thermometer calibration, 16
terminology, 3, 4, 5, 51, 53
thickeners, 37
tools and utensils
    bakeware and cookware, 2, 3
    knives, 9, 10, 11
    unusual, 98
umami, 51, 67

vegetables
    fresh vs. frozen, 58
    salad greens, 39
    rendering (sweating), 54
    substitutions, 67
    vegetarianism, 67
vinaigrette, 40

water
    how to boil, 15
    managing moisture, 54
wine, 77

Louis Eguaras is department chair at the Culinary Arts Institute at Los Angeles Mission College, Chef Instructor at the Institute of Culinary Education, and a former White House chef. He has cooked for two U.S. presidents and numerous dignitaries and celebrities, including Nelson Mandela, Tom Hanks, Anthony Hopkins, and the Rolling Stones. He lives with his wife in Newport Beach, California.

Matthew Frederick is an architect, urban designer, instructor of design and writing, and the creator of the 101 Things I Learned® series. He lives in New York's Hudson Valley.